CELEBRATE! With Fondant

Exciting, Colorful Cakes For Birthdays, Weddings And More.

Dear Friend,

Welcome to *Celebrate!® with Fondant*, the first Wilton book that is all about rolled fondant. If you've never decorated with fondant before, you are about to discover a great new way to add excitement to cakes. No icing is more fun to use. Fondant is flexible–perfect for cutting with cutters or shaping by hand. You can stamp or paint it with colorful designs, imprint it with embossed patterns or shape it into lush bows or beautiful borders. Best of all, fondant is easy for anyone to use. You can make a great-looking fondant cake your very first time. Working with fondant is so satisfying that creating a cake is as enjoyable as presenting it to the guest of honor.

Celebrate! with Fondant is the best place to see how easy and exciting fondant cakes can be. We've grouped cakes from easy to more elaborate, so you can build your fondant skills at your own pace. In every section, you will find fantastic designs which you will be proud to serve your guests. Just look at our cover cake, "Take a Bow!", for a great example of the wonderful shapes, colors and textures you can create with fondant. It's a lively combination of pastels, zigzag bows and star accents. We've taken this great look even further, with 4 easy alternate ways to decorate the same bow cake. You can decorate in neon colors, add curls to the bow or attach cut-out balloons and packages for the perfect birthday cake. With fondant, it's all up to you.

Our cover cake is just the start of the amazing cakes you will find in this inspiring book. From irresistible fondant clowns to breathtaking floral bouquets, there is a great cake for every celebration. With every idea, we'll give you options for changing the look and suggest other occasions for celebrating with that cake.

Along with great cakes, *Celebrate! with Fondant* features the tried and true step-by-step instructions you need to make decorating a breeze. Our Fondant Basics section includes everything from covering cakes with fondant to easy painting and stamping techniques. More stylized details are shown close-up right next to the cake. Also, look for a great selection of Wilton fondant products. Our innovative tools are easy for anyone to use. Combined with our ready-to-use fondant and color accents, they make decorating a great fondant cake more enjoyable than ever.

It's time to experience the fun of fondant for yourself. Let *Celebrate! with Fondant* be your guide.

Vince Naccarato

Vince Naccarato
Chairman and CEO
Wilton Industries, Inc.

Creative Director
Daniel Masini

Art Director/Cake Designer
Steve Rocco

Senior Cake Decorator
Mary Gavenda

Cake Decorators
Susan Matusiak
Debbie Friedman
Diane Knowlton
Judy Wysocki
Anne Christopher
Mark Malak

Editor/Writer
Jeff Shankman

Writers
Marita Seiler
Mary Enochs
Jessica Radzak

Copy Editor
Jane Mikis

Production Manager
Challis Yeager

Assistant Production Manager
Mary Stahulak

Graphic Design/Production
Marek/Janci Design
Seven Worldwide

Photography
Peter Rossi—PDR Productions
Seven Worldwide

Administrative Assistant
Sharon Gaeta

Product Director
Cathy Franczyk

In U.S.A.
Wilton Industries, Inc.
2240 West 75th Street
Woodridge, IL 60517

Retail Customer Orders:
Phone: 800-794-5866
Fax: 888-824-9520
Website: www.wilton.com

Class Locations:
Phone: 800-942-8881
www.wilton.com

In Canada
Wilton Industries, Canada, Ltd.
98 Carrier Drive
Etobicoke, Ontario M9W 5R1 Canada

Retail Customer Orders:
Phone: 416-679-0790
Fax: 416-679-0798

Class Locations:
Phone: 416-679-0790, x200
E-mail: classprograms@wilton.ca

Se Habla Espanol!
Para mas informacion,
Marque 800-436-5778

Table of Contents

One Cake, Five Great Looks!

When you wrap a gift, you choose the perfect paper and ribbon to match the event. With fondant, your party cake can be just as versatile! Start with our beautiful basic cake shown here, or use the specific checklists and instructions on pages 6 and 7 to create 4 other great looks!

On this page, we'll show you how to put together the basic bow cake design in 6 easy steps. It's a great look for birthdays, baby showers and even Mother's Day. But you can do so much more! Turn the page to see 4 exciting ways you can change the design. Brighten the look with neon colors. Add texture to the bow with fondant curliques and dots. Or attach different Cut-Out shapes such as square

packages and round balloons to create the perfect cake for any gift-giving occasion. Throughout *Celebrate!® with Fondant*, you'll see how versatile fondant decorating can be. For every cake, we'll give you several decorating options, and suggest the ideal occasions for serving it. With this book, you're sure to create the cake that's just right for your big event.

Take a Bow!

Here's what you'll need to make all of the cakes on the next 4 pages.
Next to each cake, you'll also see the checklist of supplies for that specific design.

Checklist for Cakes p. 5-7

- **Pans:** 8 x 2 in. Round
- **Fondant:** Fondant Ribbon Cutter/Embosser Set, Brush Set, Wide Glide™ Rolling Pin, Roll & Cut Mat, Easy-Glide Fondant Smoother, p. 114-119 (see individual instructions for Rolled Fondant needed)
- **Recipe:** Buttercream Icing, p. 101
- **Also:** Gum-Tex™, p. 119; 10 in. Round Silver Cake Base; Cake Dividing Set; Disposable Decorating Bags; cornstarch, paring knife, tissue
- **For This Cake, Add:** Ready-To-Use Rolled Fondant in White and Pastel Yellow (24 oz. each needed), Pastel Colors Fondant Multi Packs (2 pks. needed), Star Cut-Outs™, p. 114-115

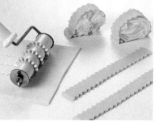

1. In advance: Make fondant bow (p. 108). Add 1/2 teaspoon of Gum-Tex each to pink, blue and green fondant from Multi Pack. Roll out fondant 1/8 in. thick and cut the following loop strips using using zigzag cutting wheels and 1/2 in. spacers from Ribbon Cutter/Embosser set (you can use 3 wheels and 2 spacers to cut

2 strips at once). Cut 4 pink, 2 green and 2 blue bow loops, 61/2 in. long and 1 green center loop, 41/2 in. long. Shape center and loops, supporting with crushed tissue and let dry. Reserve remaining fondant.

2. Prepare 2-layer round cake by icing lightly with buttercream.

3. Cover cake with 24 oz. pastel yellow fondant; smooth with Easy-Glide Smoother. Position on cake base.

4. Using Cake Dividing Set, divide cake in 8ths. Roll out reserved pink, blue and green fondant 1/8 in. thick and cut 4 pink, 2 green and 2 blue ribbon strips, 8 in. long, using Ribbon Cutter/ Embosser wheels as for loops.

Brush backs with water and attach at each cake division; trim excess.

5. Roll out 4 oz. white fondant 1/8 in. thick. Using smallest Cut-Out, cut about 56 stars. Attach between ribbon strips with damp brush.

6. Trim off corners of bow loop ends to form an outward "V" shape. Attach ends where ribbon strips meet with thinned fondant (p. 101). Attach center loop with thinned fondant. **Serves 20.**

Now that you've seen the basics of our cover cake, look here for 4 great alternative ways to decorate! You'll follow the basic steps as shown on page 4, but change the colors and trims to create the perfect design for your party.

Gifts Up for Grabs!

- **See Checklist for All Cakes,** p. 4

- **For This Cake Add:** White Ready-To-Use Rolled Fondant (24 oz.), Primary Colors Fondant Multi Pack (2 needed), Cut-Outs™ in Round and Square shapes, p. 114-115; paring knife

In advance: Follow step 1 to make 8 bow loops and 1 center loop in primary red fondant (add 1/2 teaspoon of Gum-Tex to each pack of red). Follow steps 2 and 3 to prepare cake and cover with white fondant. Follow step 4 to divide cake and cut 8 primary red strips; attach at division marks with damp brush. Roll out primary blue, yellow and green fondant 1/8 in. thick. Using smallest square and round Cut-Outs, cut packages and balloons in a variety of colors; attach to cake with damp brush. Using paring knife, cut thin strips for ribbons and balloon strings; attach with damp brush. For confetti, cut 1/4 in. squares and attach with damp brush. Follow step 6 to attach bow loops with thinned fondant. **Serves 20.**

Curly Bow

- **See Checklist for All Cakes,** p. 4

- **For This Cake, Add:** White Ready-To-Use Rolled Fondant (24 oz.), Pastel Colors Fondant Multi Pack, p. 114; Wooden Dowel Rods

In advance: Follow step 1 to make 2 bow loops each in pastel pink, blue, green and yellow and 1 center loop in green (add 1/2 teaspoon of Gum-Tex to each color). Also, using paring knife, make 4 curliques (p. 108) in each color, each 3/8 in. wide and in various lengths. Follow steps 2 and 3 to prepare cake and cover with white fondant. Follow step 4 to divide cake and cut 2 ribbon strips in each pastel color; attach with damp brush. Roll 1/4 in. diameter balls of white fondant. Attach to bow loops and ribbon strips, 1/2 in. apart, with damp brush. Follow step 6 to attach bow loops with thinned fondant; also attach curliques with thinned fondant. **Serves 20.**

2-Tone Bow

- **See Checklist for All Cakes,** p. 4
- **For This Cake, Add:** Ready-To-Use Rolled Fondant in White and Pastel Yellow (24 oz. of each), Neon Colors Fondant Multi Pack (2 needed), Round Cut-Outs™, p. 114-115

In advance: Roll out white fondant 1/8 in. thick and cut center strip for loops using 2 straight cutting wheels (without spacers) from Ribbon Cutter/Embosser. Cut strips to 61/8 in. for outside loops and 41/2 in. for center loop. Follow step 1 to make 8 bow loops and 1 center loop in neon pink fondant (add 1/2 teaspoon of Gum-Tex to each pack of pink). Attach white center strips to loop strips with damp brush and form loops. Follow steps 2 and 3 to prepare cake and cover with yellow fondant. Follow step 4 to divide cake and cut 8 neon pink ribbon strips; cut white center strips for each as on bow strips. Attach center strips to ribbons, then ribbons to cake at division marks with damp brush. Roll out orange and purple fondant 1/8 in. thick; using smallest Cut-Out, cut approximately 25 circles of each color and attach with damp brush. Follow step 6 to attach bow loops with thinned fondant.
Serves 20.

Bright with White

- **See Checklist for All Cakes,** p. 4
- **For This Cake, Add:** White Ready-To-Use Rolled Fondant (24 oz.), Pastel Colors Fondant Multi Pack, p. 114

In advance: Follow step 1 to make 2 bow loops each in neon purple, pink, orange and yellow and 1 center loop in pink (add 1/2 teaspoon of Gum-Tex to each color). Follow steps 2 and 3 to prepare cake and cover with white fondant. Follow step 4 to divide cake and cut 2 ribbon strips in each neon color; attach with damp brush. Also cut two 6 in. ribbon strips in each color, cut a "V" at outer end and attach between 8 in. strips with damp brush, 2 in. from bottom of cake. Roll 1/4 in. diameter balls of matching neon fondant for each bow loop and ribbon strip; attach 1/2 in. apart, with damp brush. Follow step 6 to attach bow loops with thinned fondant.
Serves 20.

Great Beginnings

Hit the ground running with these perfect cakes for first-time fondant users. You'll use simple techniques to make exciting designs—bright fondant balloons, wild striped candles, bugs with cut-out trims, and an elegant stamped floral heart. When decorating is this fast and fun, there's no reason to serve a plain cake!

Instructions for the cake shown here are on page 94.

Fun's Afloat

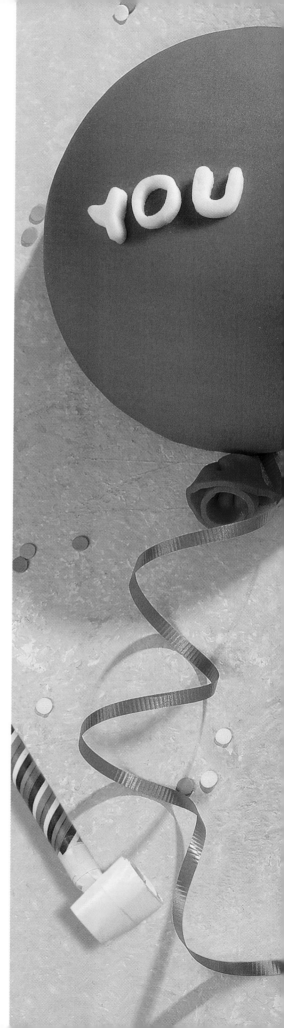

No huffing or puffing—decorating these colorful cakes is easier than blowing up a real balloon! Just cover cakes and add a twisted knot. They're perfect for personalizing with a fondant Cut-Out message.

Project Checklist

- **Pan:** Sports Ball
- **Icing Colors*:** Red-Red, Christmas Red, Royal Blue, Lemon Yellow
- **Fondant:** White Ready-To-Use Rolled Fondant (36 oz. needed), Alphabet/Number Cut-Outs, Brush Set, Wide Glide™ Rolling Pin, Roll & Cut Mat, p. 114-119
- **Recipe:** Buttercream Icing, p. 101
- **Also:** Cake Circles, Fanci-Foil Wrap, yellow, red and blue curling ribbon (2 ft. of each color needed), paring knife, ruler

Prepare 3 half ball cakes for rolled fondant by icing smooth with buttercream. Tint 12 oz. portions of fondant blue, yellow and red. Cover cakes with fondant (p. 97). For knots, roll out a small amount of each color and cut a $1^1/4$ x 3 in. long strip. Begin rolling from one end, pinching bottom together and wrapping strip loosely to form balloon knot; trim off excess. Attach to cake with damp brush. For letters, roll out white fondant $1/8$ in. thick. Cut message with Cut-Outs. Attach with damp brush. Cut and position pieces of curling ribbon beneath each cake for balloon string.

Each serves 6.

*Note: Combine Red-Red and Christmas Red for shade shown.

Perfect for These Events:
1st birthday, picnic, retirement, bon voyage

Also Try These Ideas:
Cover cakes in pastel fondant for baby showers. Personalize with messages or add star and flower cut-out shapes.

Flying Colors!

If you're just starting to decorate with fondant, our Contour Pan will be a big help. Its rounded top edge makes it easy to cover your first cake perfectly smooth.

Project Checklist

- **Pan:** 9 x 3 in. Contour, p. 118
- **Fondant:** White Ready-To-Use Rolled Fondant (24 oz.), Primary Colors Fondant Multi Pack, Cut-Outs™ in Star, Round and Flower shapes; Cutter/Embosser, Brush Set, Perfect Height™ Rolling Pin, Roll & Cut Mat, Easy-Glide Fondant Smoother, p. 114-119
- **Recipe:** Buttercream Icing, p. 101
- **Also:** 10 in. Silver Cake Base, ruler

Prepare 1-layer cake (3 in. high) for rolled fondant by icing lightly with buttercream. Cover cake with fondant; smooth with Easy-Glide Smoother. Position cake on base. Roll out primary fondant colors $1/8$ in. thick. Using medium round Cut-Outs, cut balloon circles in various colors. Using straight-edge wheel from Cutter/Embosser, cut $1/8$ x 3 in. long strips for balloon strings. Using small and medium Cut-Outs, cut yellow stars. Attach all to cake with damp brush. With Cutter/Embosser, cut five $3/4$ x 8 in. long yellow strips for bottom border; with toothpick, mark alternating points at top and bottom, $3/4$ in. apart. Using straight-edge wheel of Cutter/Embosser, emboss diagonal lines between top and bottom points to form a crisscross pattern. Attach sections to bottom border with damp brush, making gentle folds as you attach. **Serves 11.**

Perfect for These Events:
Any age birthday, baby shower, graduation

Also Try These Ideas:
Change the bottom border to fondant balls or ropes. Brighten the stars with Shimmer Dust™.

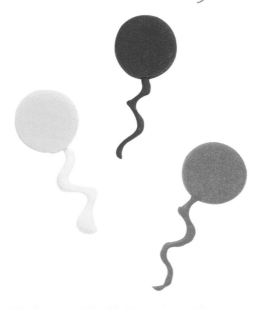

Friends Fly Together

They'll think you were busy as a bee when they see these adorable bugs. Our ball and mini ball pans make ideal insect cakes—all you do is cover with fondant, then cut out fun details like stripes, spots and wings.

Project Checklist

- **Pan:** Sports Ball, Mini Ball

- **Icing Colors:** Black, Red-Red, Christmas Red, Lemon Yellow, Leaf Green

- **Fondant:** White Ready-To-Use Rolled Fondant (48 oz. needed), Round Cut-Outs™, Fondant Ribbon Cutter/ Embosser Set, Brush Set, Perfect Height™ Rolling Pin, Roll & Cut Mat, p. 114-119

- **Recipe:** Buttercream Icing, p. 101

- **Also:** Nesting Heart Cookie Cutters, 4 in. Lollipop Sticks, Cake Board, Fanci-Foil Wrap, black shoestring licorice, small plastic ruler, craft knife, cornstarch, shredded coconut

At least 2 days in advance: Make bee's wings. Roll out white fondant $1/8$ in. thick and cut 2 wings using largest heart cutter. Trim off 1 in. from bottom of pointed end of each heart; let dry 48 hours on cornstarch-dusted surface. When completely dry, attach 2 lollipop sticks to each wing with thinned fondant (p. 101) (leave 2 in. of sticks extended to insert into cake). Let dry.

Bake and cool $1/2$ sports ball cake for each body and 1 mini ball cake for each head. Prepare cakes for rolled fondant by lightly icing with buttercream.

For Bee: Tint 12 oz. fondant yellow and 8 oz. black*. Roll out fondant and cover body with yellow and head with black (p. 97). For stripes, roll out black fondant $1/8$ in. thick; cut 11 in. long strips, using 2 zigzag wheels with $1/2$ in. spacer from Ribbon Cutter/Embosser Set. Attach strips to cake with damp brush; trim off excess. For stinger, roll $1^1/2$ in. ball of black fondant; shape a point at one end and attach to back of cake with damp brush.

For Ladybug: Tint 12 oz. fondant Red-Red/Christmas Red combination and 8 oz. black*. Cover body with red fondant and head with black. Roll out black fondant $1/8$ in. thick.

Use medium round cut-out to cut spots and attach to cake with damp brush.

Make faces: For eyes, roll two $1/2$ in. white balls and attach with damp brush; for pupils, roll $1/4$ in. black balls and attach with damp brush. For mouth, roll $1^1/2$ in. x $1/8$ in. diameter log; attach with damp brush. Roll $1/4$ in. black balls and attach for cheeks. For eyelashes, roll 2 x $3/4$ in. strips of fondant; cut slits $1/8$ in. wide x $1/2$ in. deep. Cut strips in half to make set of 2 lashes; attach to cake with damp brush. Curl lashes around brush handle. For antennas, cut two 3 in. lengths of shoestring licorice; roll $1/4$ in. black balls and attach on ends; insert into cake. Attach heads to bodies with buttercream. Insert bee's wings.
Each serves 7.

***Note:** You can also use pre-tinted black fondant from our Natural Colors Fondant Multi Pack. You will need 2 packs for each bee or ladybug.

Perfect for These Events:
Girl's birthday, garden or summer theme party, picnic

Also Try These Ideas:
Add cone-shaped fondant party hats. Make additional bug cakes for more guests.

Drum Major

You can't beat this colorful drum for an easy birthday party cake. The great zigzag side detail is made in minutes with a roll of the Ribbon Cutter/Embosser. Kids will get a bang out of the sticks, too!

Project Checklist

- **Pan:** 8 x 2 in. Round

- **Fondant:** Ready-To-Use Rolled Fondant in White and Pastel Blue, Primary Colors Fondant Multi Packs (2 pks. needed), Cut-Outs™ in Square and Alphabet/Number shapes, Fondant Ribbon Cutter/Embosser Set, Brush Set, Rolling Pin, Roll & Cut Mat, Easy-Glide Fondant Smoother, p. 114-119

- **Recipe:** Buttercream Icing, p. 101

- **Also:** Gum-Tex™, p. 119; 8 in. Cookie Treat Sticks, Cake Board, Fanci-Foil Wrap, Cake Dividing Set, paring knife

Prepare 2-layer cake for rolled fondant by lightly icing with buttercream. Cover top in white and sides in pastel blue fondant (p. 97); smooth with Easy-Glide Smoother. For rims, roll out red fondant $1/4$ in. thick and cut 2 strips, 26 in. long, using 2 straight wheels with $1/2$ in. spacer from Ribbon Cutter/Embosser Set. Attach at top and bottom borders with damp brush. Divide cake into 8ths. Roll out yellow fondant $1/8$ in. thick and cut $4 1/2$ in. long strips using 2 zigzag wheels with $1/4$ in. spacer from set. Attach strips at division marks in crisscross fashion. Cut 16 trims using primary blue fondant and smallest square Cut-Out. Cut 8 of these squares in half, from corner to corner to make triangles; attach trims between crisscross areas with damp brush. For additional trim, roll 16 green fondant balls, $5/16$ in. diameter; flatten at

bottom and attach at division points with damp brush. For name, cut blue fondant letters with Cut-Outs and attach with damp brush. For drum sticks, roll two $1 1/4$ in. diameter yellow balls; insert a cookie stick in each and position on cake top.

Serves 20.

Perfect for These Events:
1st birthday, band party, Christmas celebration

Also Try These Ideas:
Decorate trims in holiday colors. Add Cake Sparkles™ on the sides to create a metal flake effect.

Heart-Pounding Excitement!

Serving individual desserts is no trouble when you decorate with fondant. Check out all the exciting effects you can use to dazzle your guests. Our pre-tinted Fondant Multi Packs let you create a rainbow of shades in no time.

Project Checklist

- **Pan:** Mini Heart
- **Fondant:** White Ready-To-Use Rolled Fondant, Fondant Multi Packs in Neon and Primary Colors, Cut-Outs™ in Heart, Funny Flower and Round Shapes, Cutter/Embosser, Brush Set, Perfect Height™ Rolling Pin, Roll & Cut Mat, p. 114-119
- **Recipe:** Buttercream Icing, p. 101

Prepare mini heart cakes for rolled fondant by icing lightly with buttercream. Tint fondant as follows: For orange, combine 2 oz. neon orange with 2 oz. white. For blue used in dots, combine 1 oz. blue with 1 oz. white. For green, combine 1 oz. primary green and 1 oz. primary yellow with 4 oz. white. For purple heart used on green cake, combine $1/2$ oz. purple and $1/2$ oz. white fondant.

Cover cakes with neon yellow, neon pink, neon purple, orange combination and green combination fondant (p. 97). For yellow cake, cut 6 white flowers using the smallest Cut-Out; attach with damp brush. Roll $3/16$ in. balls of orange combination fondant for flower centers and attach with damp brush. For pink cake, cut $1/4$ in. wide white fondant strips with Cutter/Embosser; attach to cake in crisscross fashion, $1/4$ in. apart, with damp brush. Trim off excess fondant.

For purple cake, cut yellow heart using largest heart cutter; attach with damp brush. Cut $1/8$ in. wide pink fondant strips and attach in criss-cross fashion, $1/4$ in. apart with damp brush. Roll approximately 30 blue combination balls, $1/4$ in. diameter, and attach to sides with damp brush. For orange cake, cut pink, purple, yellow and green combination circles using smallest round Cut-Out; attach with damp brush. For green cake, cut purple combination, pink and yellow hearts using large, medium and small Cut-Outs; attach with damp brush. Roll approximately 38 balls of green combination fondant, $1/8$ in. diameter; attach with damp brush.

Each serves 1.

Perfect for These Events:
Tea party, anniversary reception, Valentine's Day, teacher gifts

Also Try These Ideas:
Use bright red or pink for Valentines, soft pastels for showers. Serve as edible place markers with names printed using FoodWriter markers.

Super-Size Wishes!

Fondant gives you freedom to use color in so many ways! Rather than celebrate with one big cake, why not break the mold with several small candle cakes that show off all the colors at your command? Light up the room with primary and neon colors in fun waves, stripes and cut-outs.

Project Checklist

- **Pan:** Mini Loaf
- **Fondant:** White Ready-To-Use Rolled Fondant (48 oz. needed), Fondant Multi Packs in Primary and Neon Colors, Cut-Outs™ in Leaf, Round, Star and Square shapes; Fondant Ribbon Cutter/Embosser Set, Brush Set, Perfect Height™ Rolling Pin, Roll & Cut Mat; Easy-Glide Fondant Smoother, p. 114-119
- **Recipe:** Buttercream Icing, p. 101
- **Also:** Gum-Tex™, p. 119; 101 Cookie Cutters Set, 4 in. Lollipop Sticks, Cake Boards, Fanci-Foil Wrap, cornstarch, paring knife

In advance: Make fondant flames and letters. For flames, mix $1/8$ teaspoon of Gum-Tex each into $1/2$ pack of neon yellow and $1/2$ pack of neon orange fondant. Use large and medium leaf Cut-Outs to cut 6 large yellow and 6 medium orange flames. Attach medium flame to large flame with damp brush; let dry completely. For letters, combine $3^1/2$ oz. of Primary Red fondant with $1/2$ teaspoon of Gum-Tex. Cut message using alphabet cookie cutters. Let letters dry on cornstarch-dusted surface. To attach flames to lollipop sticks, thread a $3/4$ x $1/4$ in. diameter log of fondant on the tip of stick. Flatten log slightly; brush with water and gently press flames on back; set aside to dry.

Bake and cool 12 mini loaf cakes. Position 6 sets of 2 cakes end to end to form 6 candles. Prepare cakes for rolled fondant by lightly icing with buttercream. Cover 3 cakes with 6 oz. each of white fondant (p. 98); smooth with Easy-Glide Smoother. Add 1 oz. white fondant to each pack of blue and green fondant. Roll out assorted colors $1/8$ in. thick and use smallest star, round and square Cut-Outs to cut shapes to decorate 3 white candles; attach shapes to cakes with damp brush.

For remaining 3 cakes, roll out 6 oz. white fondant large enough to cover each candle. Roll out assorted colors and cut as follows: For diagonal striped cake, cut strips using 2 straight wheels with $1/2$ in. spacer from Ribbon Cutter/Embosser Set. Brush white piece with water and attach colored strips; roll flat to blend into one evenly-striped piece. Cover cake, smooth and trim off excess fondant. For horizontal striped cake, repeat process, cutting assorted colors using straight wheels and 1 in. spacer. For wavy striped cake, cut yellow strips using straight wheels and $1/2$ in. spacer; cut other color strips using $1/4$ in. spacer; repeat process.

Insert lollipop stick flames into candle cakes; position message.
Each serves 2.

Perfect for These Events: Birthdays for all ages, school celebrations

Also Try These Ideas: Make 4th of July fireworks in red, white and blue. Change the message and color to suit your event.

Gentle Garden Trio

Even a plain iced cake can benefit from the texture of fondant. Garlands of blossoms and leaves look great atop pastel-iced cakes. The fondant-wrapped board is imprinted with delicate lines which lead the eye toward the cake.

Project Checklist

- **Pans:** 8 x 2 in. Square, 8 x 2 in. Heart, 8 x 2 in. Round
- **Tip:** 3
- **Icing Colors:*** Rose, Royal Blue, Lemon Yellow, Golden Yellow, Leaf Green
- **Fondant:** White Ready-to-Use Rolled Fondant (72 oz. needed), Pastel Colors Fondant Multi Pack, Flower and Leaf Cut-Outs™, Cutter/Embosser, Brush Set, Perfect Height™ Rolling Pin, Roll & Cut Mat, Easy-Glide Fondant Smoother, p. 114-119
- **Recipe:** Buttercream Icing, p.101
- **Also:** Cake Boards, Fanci-Foil Wrap, Piping Gel, ruler, cellophane tape, toothpick

Ice smooth 2-layer cakes, 3 in. high, with buttercream and place on same-size cake boards. For each cake, cut two more boards 3 in. larger than cake; tape boards together and wrap with foil. Cover boards with fondant (p. 99) and imprint following instructions below.

Roll $1/4$ in. white fondant balls for bottom borders and attach with damp brush. Roll out pastel green fondant $1/16$ in. thick and cut 170 leaves using smallest leaf Cut-Out. Roll out white fondant $1/16$ in. thick. For bottom border cut 124 flowers using smallest flower Cut-Out; for cake tops cut 24 flowers using medium flower Cut-Out. Roll small balls of pastel yellow fondant for flower centers (flatten balls for larger flowers) and attach with damp brush. Attach small flowers and leaves to border with damp brush. Position large flowers on cake tops. Pipe tip 3 vines[†] in buttercream between flowers. Position leaves on cake tops.

Round and square each serve 20; heart serves 18.

*Note: Combine Lemon Yellow and Golden Yellow for pastel yellow shade shown.

†Note: For instructions on specific piping techniques, see the Wilton Yearbook of Cake Decorating or visit www.wilton.com.

Perfect for These Events:
Bridal shower, wedding, anniversary, ladies' birthday, Mother's Day, retirement

Also Try These Ideas:
Change the flower colors to match wedding and shower colors. Create the design on other popular wedding shapes—ovals, petals and hexagons.

IMPRINTED FONDANT BOARDS

1. For each set of boards, roll out 24 oz. fondant $1/8$ in. thick. Cover taped, foil-covered boards with fondant (p. 99); smooth with Easy-Glide Smoother. Reserve remaining fondant.

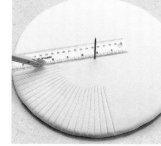

2. Mark center with toothpick. Using ruler as a guide and straight-edge wheel of Cutter/Embosser, imprint lines $3/8$ in. apart, starting from edge of board and moving toward center.

3. Position cakes and decorate following instructions.

Party Big Time!

No quiet cupcakes here! These are over the top—jumbo in size and attitude. Just cover with fondant, add the fun little trims and top with a mountain of buttercream.

Project Checklist

- **Pan:** Jumbo Muffin

- **Tip:** 1M

- **Fondant:** Pastel Yellow Ready-To-Use Rolled Fondant, Fondant Multi Packs in Neon and Primary Colors, Round Cut-Outs™, Cutter/Embosser, Brush Set, Perfect Height™ Rolling Pin, Roll & Cut Mat, Easy-Glide Fondant Smoother, p. 114-119

- **Recipe:** Buttercream Icing, p. 101

- **Also:** Cake Release, small plastic ruler

Lightly coat muffin pan cavities with Cake Release; bake and cool cupcakes. Prepare cupcakes for rolled fondant by turning over and lightly icing bottoms and sides with buttercream. Cover bottoms and sides with yellow fondant (p. 97); smooth with Easy-Glide Smoother. Turn upright, lightly ice tops with buttercream and smooth edges of fondant. For stripes, roll assorted fondant colors $1/8$ in. thick and cut $3/8$ x 2 in. long strips; attach to sides with damp brush. For dots, cut assorted fondant colors with smallest round Cut-Out; attach to sides with damp brush. For spirals, roll assorted fondant colors into $1/8$ in. diameter rope; shape into spirals and attach to sides with damp brush. In buttercream, pipe tip 1M swirls in a circular motion on cupcake tops. Roll $3/4$ in. diameter balls of red fondant for cherries and position on cupcake tops.
Each serves 1.

Perfect for These Events:
School treats, kids' birthday

Also Try These Ideas:
Top each with a birthday candle. Use flower or star Cut-Outs to decorate sides. Add Cake Sparkles™ to tops.

One Great Freight

Now your fondant skills are picking up steam. You know how to engineer simple loaf cakes into a classic train shape, which is ready to top with bright fondant trims. Add the birthday message in a trail of fondant smoke.

Project Checklist

- **Pans:** 9 x 5 in. Loaf, Standard Muffin
- **Tips:** Any standard tip, any large tip with 1 in. bottom
- **Icing Colors:** Royal Blue, Black
- **Fondant:** Ready-To-Use Rolled Fondant in White and Pastel Blue, Primary Colors Fondant Multi Packs (2 pks. needed); Cut-Outs™ in Square and Alphabet/Number shapes; Cutter/ Embosser, Brush Set, Perfect Height™ Rolling Pin, Roll & Cut Mat, Easy-Glide Fondant Smoother, p. 114-119
- **Recipe:** Buttercream Icing, p. 101
- **Also:** 101 Cookie Cutters Set or make circle patterns of 2³/4 and 4³/4 in., Cake Boards, Fanci-Foil Wrap, cornstarch

In advance: Make fondant wheels. Tint 6 oz. white fondant black. Roll out ¹/8 in. thick and cut 1 large and 2 medium wheels using large and medium round cutters from set or cut using 4³/4 and 2³/4 in. circle patterns. Roll eight ¹/8 in. wide strips for spokes on each wheel; attach with damp brush. Roll a ¹/4 in. wide log for wheel rim and attach around edge of wheel with damp brush. For wheel centers, roll out yellow fondant ¹/4 in. thick and cut circles using wide end of standard tip for medium wheels and wide end of large tip for large wheel; attach with damp brush. For wheel bars, roll a ³/8 in. diameter green log; cut 5 in. and 3 in. lengths; let dry on cornstarch-dusted surface.

Bake two 9 x 5 in. loaf cakes (2 in. high) and one cupcake. Assemble train following instructions below. Prepare cakes for rolled fondant by icing lightly with buttercream. Add royal blue icing color to pastel blue fondant. Place loaf cakes on same size boards; cover with fondant (p. 98) and smooth with Easy-Glide Smoother. Cover cupcake with green fondant; cut a ¹/8 in. wide strip of yellow fondant and attach around top edge with damp brush. Position cakes on shaped board. Using large square Cut-Out, cut a white fondant window; attach to cabin with damp brush. Roll ¹/4 in. diameter green logs—two 2 in. long and two

2³/4 in. long; attach for window frame with damp brush. Roll a 1 x 10 in. log of yellow fondant; attach for cabin roof with damp brush. Roll out red fondant ¹/4 in. thick and cut three ³/4 x 4¹/2 in. long strips for engine trim; attach with damp brush, placing one where cakes meet. Roll and flatten a 1 in. yellow ball headlight; attach. For cowcatcher, roll out green fondant ³/4 in. thick and cut a triangle with a 2¹/4 in. vertical side and a 1¹/4 in. horizontal side, cut a diagonal side to meet ends. Imprint lines with straight-edge wheel of Cutter/Embosser; attach with damp brush. Attach wheels and wheel bars with damp brush. Roll various size balls of white fondant; position in a trail from smokestack. Cut message letters from red fondant using Cut-Outs; position on cake and smoke balls. **Serves 10.**

Perfect for These Events:
Boy's birthday, train buff's birthday

Also Try These Ideas:
Add more cars for larger parties. Decorate in holiday colors for a festive Christmas train.

ASSEMBLING TRAIN CAKE

1. Cut 1 loaf cake to 6 in. long; level cupcake to 1¹/4 in. high. Assemble cakes on large plain board, positioning 9 in. cake vertically for engineer's cabin, 6 in. cake horizontally for engine front and cupcake for smokestack. Trace train shape on board, adding area for cowcatcher and cabin roof. Cut train pattern from board, wrap with foil.

2. Position cakes on same-size cake boards. Prepare and cover cakes with rolled fondant.

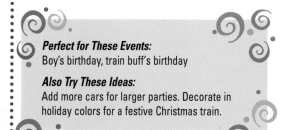

3. Reposition cakes on shaped board and add fondant trims.

Hearts Entwined

If you've never stamped a cake before, you've missed an exciting way to decorate. It's a great tapestry look that only happens with fondant— and it's easy with our Brush-On Color™ and Cake Stamps™.

Project Checklist

- **Pans:** 6 x 2 in.and 10 x 2 in. Heart
- **Tip:** 2
- **Icing Colors:** Rose, White-White
- **Fondant:** White Ready-To-Use Rolled Fondant (48 oz. needed), Brush Set, Brush-On Color™ in Pink and Green, Nature Cake Stamps™, Color Tray, Perfect Height™ Rolling Pin, Roll & Cut Mat, Easy-Glide Fondant Smoother, p. 114-119
- **Recipe:** Buttercream Icing, p. 101
- **Also:** Cake Board, Fanci-Foil Wrap, Professional Turntable, cornstarch, paring knife

In advance: Make fondant center heart. Tint 2 oz. white fondant rose. Roll out $1/4$ in. thick and position 6 in. heart pan, bottom side up, on top. Cut heart shape using paring knife. Place heart on cornstarch-dusted surface to dry.

Prepare 2-layer 10 in. cake for rolled fondant by lightly icing with buttercream. Cover cake with fondant (p. 98); smooth with Easy-Glide Smoother. In Color Tray, combine pink Brush-On Color with White-White Icing Color; repeat using green Brush-On Color and White-White Icing Color. Place cake on turntable so you can stamp partial designs at bottom edge. Stamp 3 or 4 flowers at a time onto cake, using 6-petal flower stamp and pink mixture (stir mixture before each stamp). Paint green stems using round brush. Stamp leaves on stems using leaf stamp and green mixture (stir mixture before each stamp). Continue stamping and painting to cover entire cake.

Position cake on serving plate or foil-wrapped board cut slightly larger than cake. Roll two $1/4$ in. diameter ropes, twist together and attach at bottom border with damp brush. Using rose buttercream and tip 2, write message* on center heart. Attach to cake with buttercream.

Serves 24.

*Note: For instructions on specific piping techniques, see the Wilton Yearbook of Cake Decorating or visit www.wilton.com.

Perfect for These Events:
Bridal shower, small wedding, anniversary, ladies' birthday, Mother's Day, Valentine's Day

Also Try These Ideas:
Stamp on red flowers for Valentine's Day or other shades to match reception colors.

Address the Ball!

This is a "gimme"—a perfect cake for any golfer that's as easy as a 1 foot putt, thanks to rolled fondant. Simply cover the cake, imprint the dimples and shape your tee. A great way to celebrate, while staying out of the rough!

Project Checklist

- **Pan:** 10 x 2 in. Round
- **Icing Color:** Red-Red
- **Fondant:** White Ready-To-Use Rolled Fondant (48 oz. needed), Alphabet/Number Cut-Outs™, Wide Glide™ Rolling Pin, Roll & Cut Mat, Easy-Glide Fondant Smoother, p. 114-119
- **Recipe:** Buttercream Icing, p. 101
- **Also:** Confectionery Tool Set, p. 118; Cake Board, Fanci-Foil Wrap, cornstarch

Prepare 1-layer cake for rolled fondant by icing lightly with buttercream. Cover cake with fondant, about $1/4$ to $3/8$ in. thick; smooth with Easy-Glide Smoother. To make dimples, imprint cake with medium ball tool from confectionery set, dusting end of tool with cornstarch to prevent sticking. Tint approximately 12 oz. of fondant red. Make message using Cut-Outs and red fondant. Shape a $4^1/2$ x $1^3/4$ x 1 in. deep piece for base of tee; shape a piece for spike of tee measuring 5 x 2 x $5/8$ in. deep and tapering to $1/2$ x 1 in. wide. Position at bottom of ball cake. Position message.
Serves 14.

Perfect for These Events:
Birthday, retirement party, Father's Day, golf tournament

Also Try These Ideas:
Add name, event or date with fondant Cut-Outs, decorate a company logo in buttercream, change tee colors, make additional golf balls for larger groups.

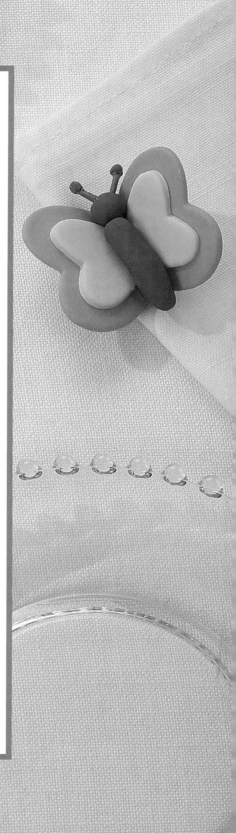

Building on the Basics

You're ready to take the next step in fondant decorating! Make your first textured bows with the Ribbon Cutter/Embosser tool— and use them to top a pretty trio of pastel gift package cakes. Also explore elegant hand-shaped trims such as ruffles and swags, and fun hand-cut accents like the blossom-loving butterflies shown here. You'll be amazed at how easy a great-looking fondant cake can be!

Instructions for the cake shown here are on page 94.

Our Newest Star

Wake up the baby cake with some fun shapes! Cake Stamps are the perfect solution—just dip them in Brush-On Color, stamp them on your cake or Cut-Outs and add Shimmer Dust for extra color and sparkle.

Project Checklist

- **Pan:** Star

- **Icing Color:** White-White

- **Fondant:** Ready-To-Use Rolled Fondant in Pastel Yellow (48 oz. needed) and White (24 oz. needed), Pastel Colors Fondant Multi Pack (2 pks. needed), Brush-On Color™ in Green, Pink, Orange, Blue and Yellow, Baby and Romantic Cake Stamps™, Color Tray, Bright Shimmer Dust™, Brush Set, Wide Glide™ Rolling Pin, Roll & Cut Mat, Easy-Glide Fondant Smoother, p. 114-119

- **Recipe:** Buttercream Icing, p. 101

- **Also:** Gum-Tex™, p. 119; Duck Pattern, p. 112; Nesting Stars Metal Cutter Set, Wooden Dowel Rods, 4 in. Lollipop Sticks, Cake Board, Fanci-Foil Wrap, cornstarch, craft knife

In advance: Make fondant bow (p. 108). Mix 2 pks. of pastel blue from Multi Packs with 2 oz. white fondant; add $3/4$ teaspoon Gum-Tex for firmness (reserve 3 oz. of mixture for stars and bow ring). Roll out $1/8$ in. thick and cut two 3 x 11 in. bow loop strips, two $1^1/4$ x 7 in. streamer strips; bow center will be replaced by bow ring. Let pieces dry for 24 hours on cornstarch-dusted surface. Do not complete bow assembly until cake is decorated. For bow ring, make a $3/4$ x $4^1/2$ in. long log from reserved blue fondant and shape over a point on Star Pan. Cut 2 lollipop sticks to 3 in. long; brush water on ends and insert 1 in. into ends of bow ring. Let dry. For fondant stars, use 1 pk. each of yellow, pink and green from Multi Packs, each mixed with $1/2$ teaspoon of Gum-Tex. Roll out colors plus reserved blue mixture, $1/8$ in. thick and cut stars using smallest and 2nd smallest cutters. For large base stars mix 6 oz. white fondant with $1/4$ teaspoon Gum-Tex. Roll out $1/8$ in. thick and cut stars using 3rd smallest cutter. Attach 2nd smallest stars to white stars with damp brush and let all stars dry. For curls, add $1/2$ teaspoon Gum-Tex to 2 oz. pink fondant; roll out $1/8$ in. thick and cut $1/4$ x 9 in. long strips. Wrap strips around dowel rod, let set a few minutes, then slide off onto cornstarch-dusted board. Let dry.

Prepare cake for rolled fondant by icing lightly with buttercream. Cover cake with yellow fondant (p. 98); smooth with Easy-Glide Smoother. Stamp swirl designs using Romantic Cake Stamp and yellow Brush-On Color. Sprinkle swirls with Shimmer Dust; brush off excess. Roll out yellow fondant $1/4$ in. thick and cut out duck using pattern. Using Brush-On Color, paint beak, wing and eye; position on cake. For designs on stars, lighten blue and pink Brush-On Color with a little White-White Icing Color; add a little yellow Brush-On Color to green. Stamp designs in center of stars with white bases using Baby Cake Stamps. Insert bow ring in cake top and secure with thinned fondant. Position bow loops, streamers, curls and stars. **Serves 12.**

Perfect for These Events:
Baby shower, 1st birthday

Also Try These Ideas:
For 1st birthdays, remove the bow and change the center shape to a bear or sailboat.

Sunshine Stems

Just as your favorite vase makes flowers look even prettier, the elegant white fondant backdrop brings out the beauty of this floral cake. Its pulled and frayed edges create the look of fine handmade paper.

Project Checklist

- **Pan:** 10 x 2 in. Square

- **Icing Color:** Kelly Green

- **Fondant:** Ready-To-Use Rolled Fondant in White (48 oz. needed) and Pastel Yellow (24 oz. needed), Neon Colors Fondant Multi Pack, Flower and Leaf Cut-Outs™, Fine Tip Neon Colors FoodWriter™, Cutter/Embosser, Brush Set, Wide Glide™ Rolling Pin, Roll & Cut Mat, Easy-Glide Fondant Smoother, p. 114-119

- **Recipe:** Buttercream Icing, p. 101

- **Also:** Cake Board, Fanci-Foil Wrap

Prepare 2-layer cake (bake two $1^1/2$ in. layers to create a 3 in. high cake) for rolled fondant by icing lightly with buttercream. Combine 24 oz. each of white and yellow fondant. Cover cake (p. 98) and smooth with Easy-Glide Smoother, reserving excess fondant. Roll out remaining white fondant and cut an 8 in. square; reserve excess fondant. Pull out edges of square between your finger and thumb to create frayed look. Attach to cake top with damp brush.

Combine 1 in. balls of pink, orange and purple fondant with 1 in. balls of white. Roll out $1/8$ in. thick. Using large Cut-Out, cut 1 flower in each color for cake top. Using smallest Cut-Out, cut 5 flowers each in yellow, pink, orange and purple for cake sides; set aside. Cut a small white flower for center of each large flower; attach with damp brush. Using black FoodWriter, outline large flowers and draw flower center lines on all small flowers. Roll $1/8$ in. yellow balls for flower centers and attach with damp brush. For leaves and vines, tint a 2 in. ball of white

fondant green. Roll out $1/8$ in. thick and cut one $1/8$ x $4^1/2$ in. stem, two $1/8$ x 3 in. stems and 11 leaves for cake top using medium Cut-Out. Reserve remainder of green for bottom border. Outline leaves and draw center line on stems with black FoodWriter. Attach to cake with damp brush. For cake sides, cut a 1 in. wide white band and attach with damp brush. Cut $1/8$ in. wide green vines and attach with damp brush. Attach small flowers with damp brush. Using smallest Cut-Out, cut 35 leaves and attach with damp brush.
Serves 15.

Perfect for These Events:
Wedding shower, female birthday, Mother's Day, anniversary

Also Try These Ideas:
Choose your guest of honor's favorite colors and styles of flowers. Add a large fondant blossom to cupcake tops to echo your cake.

Flat Out Fun!

We're taking the 3-tiered cake to a whole new level—flat against your cake table. The fondant swags, stripes and upright cake board help create the illusion of a stacked, high-rise cake.

Project Checklist

- **Pans:** 6, 8, 10 x 2 in. Square

- **Icing Colors*:** Golden Yellow, Lemon Yellow, Rose, Royal Blue, Violet, Leaf Green, Orange, Red-Red

- **Fondant:** White Ready-To-Use Rolled Fondant (144 oz. needed), Cut-Outs™ in Round, Star and Leaf Shapes, Cutter/Embosser, Brush Set, Wide Glide™ Rolling Pin, Roll & Cut Mat, Easy-Glide Fondant Smoother, p. 114-119

- **Recipe:** Buttercream Icing, p. 101

- **Also:** Gum-Tex™, p. 119; 6 in. Lollipop Sticks, Cake Boards, Fanci-Foil Wrap, All-Purpose Decorating Gloves, cornstarch, toothpick

In advance: Make fondant stars, flames and candles. Tint fondant as follows: 12 oz. violet, 36 oz. green, 48 oz. blue and 16 oz. each pink, yellow and orange. Cut 12 yellow stars using medium Cut-Out and 6 yellow flames using small leaf Cut-Out. Let dry on cornstarch-dusted surface. For candles, roll out various colors of fondant $1/8$ in. thick and wrap around 6 lollipop sticks, leaving 2 in. at bottom uncovered. Let dry.

Prepare 1-layer 6 in. cake, 2-layer 8 in. cake (3 in. high) and 2-layer 10 in. cake (4 in. high) for rolled fondant by lightly icing with buttercream. Cover 10 in. cake, $1/2$ with blue fondant, $1/2$ with green (p. 98). Cut $1/4$ x 6 in. strips of violet fondant and attach to green portion with damp brush. Cut blue circles using smallest round Cut-Out; attach with damp brush. Repeat this decorating process using orange and green for 8 in. cake and blue and pink for 6 in. cake. Divide cake tops in thirds with toothpick.

To make swags, add $1/2$ teaspoon of Gum-Tex to each portion of remaining blue, green and pink fondant. Roll out each color $1/8$ in. thick and cut each into three 5 x $3^1/2$ in. rectangles. Gather short sides into 3 pleats. Attach swags with damp brush, where color halves meet; trim as needed for each cake size. Make additional swags for cake sides, trimming to fit height of cake. Attach with damp brush. For cake base, cut a 4 x 11 in. long piece of double-thick cake board. Cover board with yellow fondant (p. 99). Attach stars to swags, flames to candles and fondant cake base to 10 in. cake side using thinned fondant. Insert candles into top side of 6 in. cake.

Serves 46.

*Note: For orange shade used, combine orange with a little red; for yellow shade used, combine lemon yellow and golden yellow.

Perfect for These Events:
Any age birthday, 4th of July, graduation celebration, awards banquet

Also Try These Ideas:
Decorate in red, white and blue for the 4th of July, decorate in white with color trims for weddings.

Safely Delivered

Everything you could want in a baby shower cake, the stork delivers! It's adorable, of course, in fun colors that work for boys or girls. Plus, it's easy as can be, with fondant-covered cakes, cupcake and cone, all connected by dowel rod neck and legs.

Project Checklist

- **Pans:** First and Ten Football, Sports Ball, Jumbo Muffin

- **Icing Colors:** Leaf Green, Lemon Yellow, Copper (skintone), Sky Blue, Pink, Orange

- **Fondant:** White Ready-To-Use Rolled Fondant (72 oz. needed), Cutter/Embosser, Bold Tip Primary FoodWriter™, Brush Set, Wide Glide™ Rolling Pin, Roll & Cut Mat, Easy-Glide Fondant Smoother, p. 114-119

- **Recipe:** Buttercream Icing, p. 101

- **Also:** Stork Wing Pattern, p. 113, Plastic Dowel Rods (3 needed), Cake Boards, Fanci-Foil Wrap, sugar ice cream cone, small plastic ruler, toothpick, craft knife

Tint fondant, making 6 oz. yellow, 3 oz. copper, 1 oz. pink and 8 oz. each orange, green and blue. For hat, trim top off jumbo muffin, then trim $1^1/2$ in. from one side. Prepare muffin, sports ball half and football cake for rolled fondant by icing lightly with buttercream. Cover muffin with blue and cakes with white fondant (p. 97); smooth with Easy-Glide Fondant Smoother.

Roll out white fondant $3/8$ in. thick; trace wing pattern and cut with craft knife. Smooth out edges and attach to football body with damp brush. Cut one dowel rod to 6 in. for neck, cut two to 8 in. for legs. Cover neck in white and legs in yellow fondant. For feet, divide orange fondant in half; roll into two 6 in. logs. Flatten logs slightly to $1^1/2$ in. wide and shape to form feet. Attach feet together with damp brush, layering so that top foot is $1/2$ in. to right of back foot. Insert legs into body; position feet to join legs. For beak, cover sugar cone with yellow fondant; using straight-edge wheel of Cutter/Embosser, mark a line for beak opening. Cut a dowel rod to 7 in. and insert 3 in. into half ball cake head; position beak over extended 4 in. of dowel rod and press into cake. Roll a 1 in. white fondant ball and position for eye; draw pupil with black FoodWriter. For hat brim, roll 3 oz. of blue fondant into a 5 in. long log. Flatten and shape to form a $1^1/2$ in. wide brim. Position brim at top of head; position hat. Roll out

pink fondant and cut a 5 x $1/8$ x $3/8$ in. wide strip for hat band. Attach with damp brush.

For baby, roll 2 oz. of copper fondant into a ball head. Roll two $1/4$ in. balls for ears, indent at center and attach with damp brush; reserve remainder. Draw eyes and mouth with black FoodWriter. For bundle, roll a portion of green fondant 1 in. thick and shape into a 5 x 4 $1/2$ in. wide triangle; round off edges. For feet, divide remaining copper fondant in half, reserving $1/8$ oz. for toes. Roll two logs $3/4$ x $1^1/2$ in. long and flatten slightly. Roll $1/16$ in. ball toes and attach with damp brush. Attach head and feet to bundle with damp brush. Cut two 1 in. wide green triangles for bundle ties and attach to beak with damp brush. Cut boards to fit each cake and position cakes. For tail, roll a $1/2$ in. diameter white log; cut into various lengths from $1^1/2$ to 2 in. long and taper pieces into large teardrops. Position pieces, layering to create a fan shape. Insert neck in head and body cakes; position baby bundle. **Serves 18.**

Perfect for These Events: Baby shower, birdwatching club meeting

Also Try These Ideas: For twins, add another bundle of joy under the wing.

Making the Perfect Choice

For the couple who knows how to compromise—a cake to please everyone. It's less formal, more fun, with enough colors to work with any reception theme. The cut-out tiers are easy to decorate right on the side of the cake.

Project Checklist

- **Pans:** 6, 9 x 2 in. Round
- **Tips:** 1, 2, 3
- **Icing Colors:** Violet, Rose, Kelly Green, Lemon Yellow, Brown
- **Fondant:** Ready-To-Use Rolled Fondant in White (24 oz. needed) and Pastel Blue (48 oz. needed), Natural Colors Fondant Multi Pack, Cut-Outs™ in People, Heart, Flower and Square shapes, Cutter/Embosser, Fine Tip Primary Colors FoodWriter™, Brush Set, Wide Glide™ Rolling Pin, Roll & Cut Mat, Easy-Glide Fondant Smoother, p. 114-119
- **Recipe:** Buttercream Icing, p.101
- **Also:** Gum-Tex™, p. 119; 6 in. Lollipop Sticks, Cake Boards, Fanci-Foil Wrap, Piping Gel, Dowel Rods, Parchment Triangles, cornstarch

In advance: Make bride and groom using People Cut-Outs. For groom, using black fondant, cut shoes and pants; cut tuxedo jacket using shirt Cut-Out. Cut out two small triangles for bow tie. Pull down body and arms of tuxedo jacket to elongate. Cut a "V" shape from tuxedo and replace with same size "V" cut from white fondant for shirt. Cut two lapel shapes with notches. For bride, using white fondant, cut blouse. For skirt, roll fondant thin and cut a 2 x 2¹/2 in. piece; gather long edge to form pleats, adjust width to fit bottom of blouse. Cut both heads using natural pink fondant. For groom, cut 2 hands using shoe Cut-Out, cut in half leaving rounded part. For bride, cut a sliver of pink for neckline using head Cut-Out. Cut 2 pink arms using shoe Cut-Out; bend slightly. Allow all pieces to dry on cornstarch-dusted surface.

When pieces are dry, attach together with thinned fondant (p.101). Attach one lollipop stick to back of each figure. For veil, roll out fondant thin and cut a 2 in.

square; gather one edge and attach to top of bride's head. Add facial features using black FoodWriter. Using buttercream, add tip 1 white dot shirt buttons, pink spiral flowers, and pull-out dot leaves. Add tip 2 swirl and string hair and white dot necklace and sleeve trim†. Let all dry.

Tint blue fondant periwinkle using violet icing color. Prepare 2-layer cakes for stacked construction (p. 99); prepare cakes for rolled fondant; cover cakes and smooth (p. 97).

For sides of 6 in. cake, make 2 each of 4 fondant cake designs. For all, use various sizes of square Cut-Outs to cut tiers in colors indicated; trim to desired sizes. Attach immediately to cake sides with damp brush, then decorate as follows: Decorate 3-tiered rose cake with pink heart, (cut with smallest Cut-Out), thin white fondant strips and tip 2 bead bottom borders in buttercream. Decorate 2-tiered white cake with yellow fondant heart, (cut with smallest Cut-Out), tip 2 green stripes and tip 1 sotas flowers in buttercream; add tip 1 pull-out leaves. Decorate 3-tiered white cake with tip 1 dot flower spray and outline "double drop strings"; add tip 1 dots at string points. Add tip 2 bead bottom borders. Decorate 3-tiered

violet cake using ¹/4 in. wide white fondant strips for pillars. Use smallest Cut-Out for violet fondant flower; add tip 1 dot center. Cut white fondant scallop trims; add tip 1 outline "drop strings".

For sides of 9 in. cake, make 2 each of 5 fondant cake designs. Repeat process for cutting and attaching tiers; for 3-tiered white cake, use straight-edge wheel of Cutter/Embosser to imprint crisscross design before attaching to cake. Decorate 3-tiered pink cake like 3-tiered white cake above, using tip 1 zigzag swags instead of outline "drop strings". Decorate 3-tiered green cake with tip 3 ball bells; add tip 1 string bow and dots on cake sides, tip 2 swirls and dot bottom borders. Decorate white cake with pink fondant heart, (cut with smallest Cut-Out); add tip 1 spiral motion flowers and pull-out leaves. Decorate 2-tiered yellow cake using ¹/4 in. wide white fondant strips for pillars. Attach yellow fondant flower, (cut with smallest Cut-Out); add tip 1 dot center. Pipe tip 2 stripes and dot bottom border. Decorate 4-tiered violet cake with tip 1 sotas flowers and pull-out leaves.

Prepare fondant ruffle on board: Cover two 12 in. cake circles with Fanci-Foil Wrap. Knead ¹/4 teaspoon Gum-Tex into 6 oz. white fondant. Roll out fondant thin and cut 2 in. wide strips. Brush edge of board lightly with piping gel; gather one edge of each strip into pleats and attach to board. Position cakes. Insert bride and groom into cake top. Pipe tip 3 dot borders between cake designs in buttercream.

Serves 32.*

*****Note:** The top tier is often saved for the first anniversary. The number of servings given does not include top tier.

†**Note:** For instructions on specific piping techniques, see the Wilton Yearbook of Cake Decorating or visit www.wilton.com.

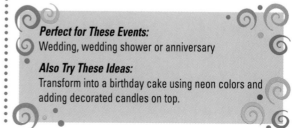

Perfect for These Events:
Wedding, wedding shower or anniversary

Also Try These Ideas:
Transform into a birthday cake using neon colors and adding decorated candles on top.

Three's a Charm

This cake trio seems to rise up to greet your guests!
It features 3 styles of full textured fondant bows
along with deeply cupped daisies in pretty pastels.

Project Checklist

- **Pans:** 6, 8 x 2 in. Square
- **Icing Color:** Creamy Peach
- **Fondant:** Ready-To-Use Rolled Fondant in White (24 oz. needed), Pastel Pink and Pastel Yellow (48 oz. each needed), Daisy Cut-Outs™, Fondant Ribbon Cutter/Embosser Set, Brush Set, Wide Glide™ Rolling Pin, Roll & Cut Mat, Easy-Glide Fondant Smoother, p. 114-119
- **Recipe:** Buttercream Icing, p. 101
- **Also:** Candy Melting Plate, p. 118; Gum-Tex™, p. 119; Cake Board, Fanci-Foil Wrap, cornstarch, paring knife, facial tissue

In advance: Make fondant bow pieces using 12 oz. white fondant with 1 teaspoon of Gum-Tex added for firmness. Roll out fondant $3/16$ in. thick and cut pieces using Ribbon Cutter/Embosser. For pink cake, use straight-edge cutters and 2 beaded embossing wheels with 1 in. spacer. For yellow cake, use straight-edge cutters and 2 striped embossing wheels (no spacer). For peach cake, use wavy-edge cutters with 1 in. spacer. For each pink and yellow cake, cut two 10 in. strips for loops and one $3^{1}/2$ in. strip for center (p. 108). For peach cake, cut two 7 in. strips for loops and one 3 in. strip for center. Support loops with crushed tissue. Let dry on cornstarch-dusted surface. Reserve remaining fondant.

Prepare 3-layer 6 in. cake (two 2 in. and one 1 in. high to make 5 in. high cake), 2-layer 8 in. cake (3 in. high) and 1-layer 6 in. cake (2 in. high) for rolled fondant by lightly icing with buttercream. Combine 12 oz. pink with 4 oz. yellow fondant, then add peach icing color to make the deep peach color. Cover 5 in. high cake with yellow, 3 in. high cake with pink and 2 in. high cake with peach fondant (p. 98); smooth with Easy-Glide Smoother.

Make flowers using remaining fondant from cakes. Roll fondant $1/16$ in. thick and use medium daisy Cut-Out to cut 43 yellow, 36 pink and 20 peach flowers. Let dry in candy melting plate cavities, dusted with cornstarch, to create a cupped shape. Roll $1/8$ in. balls of white fondant and attach to center of flowers with damp brush; gently press to flatten ball. Let dry.

Make additional bow pieces from reserved white fondant, using same Cutter/Embosser wheels as before. For yellow cake, cut four 8 in. ribbon strips and two $5^{1}/2$ in. streamers. Cut "V" shapes at end of streamers. Immediately attach 2 ribbon strips with damp brush, starting at center bottom of opposite cake sides and working toward center; repeat for other 2 strips, trimming off excess at top. Attach streamers and bow center with damp brush. Insert loops, securing with thinned fondant. For pink cake, cut four 7 in. ribbons and two $5^{1}/2$ in. streamers; for peach cake, cut four 7 in. ribbons and two 4 in. streamers. Attach pieces as for yellow cake.

Randomly attach flowers to cake sides and top with thinned fondant (p. 101).

Yellow cake serves 20, pink cake serves 10, peach cake serves 6.

Perfect for These Events:
Female birthday for all ages, wedding, shower

Also Try These Ideas:
To decorate as a general celebration cake, replace flowers with balloon or star trims. Change colors for Christmas gifts.

Booming Out the Tunes

Here's how you pump up the volume on a plain loaf cake. Stack 2 cakes together, cover with fondant and add fondant controls, speakers, handle and discs for a party cake that's a blast.

Project Checklist

- **Pan:** Long Loaf

- **Tip:** One standard and one large size decorating tip

- **Icing Colors:** Black, Royal Blue

- **Fondant:** White Ready-To-Use Rolled Fondant (72 oz. needed), Neon Colors Fondant Multi Pack, Cutter/Embosser, Brush Set, Perfect Height™ Rolling Pin, Roll & Cut Mat, Easy-Glide Fondant Smoother, p. 114-119

- **Recipe:** Buttercream Icing, p. 101

- **Also:** Display Panel Pattern, p. 112, 101 Cookie Cutters Set, Cake Board, Fanci-Foil Wrap, 4 in. Lollipop Sticks, Dowel Rods, cornstarch

In advance: Make boom box handle, controls, discs and speakers. For handle, tint 48 oz. fondant blue. Roll a log, $3/4$ in. diameter x 15 in. long; reserve remaining blue fondant. Bend ends of log down starting $2^1/2$ in. from each end. Insert a lollipop stick 1 in. deep into each end; let dry on cornstarch-dusted surface. For disc centers and speakers, tint 6 oz. fondant gray and 6 oz. black. Roll out black, gray and neon fondant $1/8$ in. thick; using largest round cutter, cut black speakers and neon color discs. Score speakers with vertical and horizontal lines using ridged wheel of Cutter/Embosser. Using smallest round cutter, cut center out of discs and replace with same-size gray fondant circle. Insert lollipop stick to cut center hole in discs; let discs and speakers dry on cornstarch-dusted surface. For round boombox dials, cut circles using large opening of decorating tip. For buttons, cut five rectangles, $5/8$ x $1/4$ in. and two $7/8$ x $1/2$ in. Cut a $4^1/2$ x $1^1/2$ in. rectangle for dial bar and a $4^1/2$ x $3/4$ in. rectangle for disc input bar. Using a lollipop stick, indent disc input bar and fill in with black fondant strip for disc opening. Using pattern, cut display panel. Let all pieces dry on cornstarch-dusted surface.

Stack two 3 in. high long loaf cakes; insert dowel rods to secure. Prepare cakes for rolled fondant by lightly icing with buttercream. Cover with remaining blue fondant (p. 98) and smooth with Easy-Glide Smoother. Attach fondant pieces to cake with damp brush. For handle holders, roll gray fondant $1/4$ in. thick and cut 2 circles using smallest round cutter. Indent center of holders with end of rolling pin. Position holders on top of cake and insert handle. Position discs.
Serves 24.

Perfect for These Events:
Birthday, school band party, kids' dance party

Also Try These Ideas:
Cover boombox with any color you like. Add messages or names on discs with Icing Writer.

Daisies Go Crazy!

With fondant, eye-popping color combinations seem totally natural. The layered flowers create bursts of brightness that tell everyone it's time to have fun. This cake also brings smooth and ridged textures together for a unique statement.

Project Checklist

- **Pan:** 6 x 2 in. Round

- **Icing Colors:** Royal Blue, Kelly Green, Violet

- **Fondant:** White Ready-To-Use Rolled Fondant (72 oz. needed), Neon Colors Fondant Multi Pack, Cut-Outs™ in Daisy and Leaf shapes, Fondant Ribbon Cutter/Embosser Set, White Icing Writer™, Shimmer Dust™ in Primary, Bright and Elegant colors, Perfect Height™ Rolling Pin, Roll & Cut Mat, p. 114-119

- **Recipe:** Buttercream Icing, p. 101

- **Also:** Plastic Dowel Rods, Cake Board, Fanci-Foil Wrap; 22-gauge cloth-covered florist wire, cornstarch

At least 2-3 days in advance: Make fondant flowers and leaves. Roll out neon fondant colors $1/8$ in. thick and cut 11 each medium and large flowers using daisy Cut-Outs. Tint 1 oz. white fondant green, roll $1/8$ in. thick and cut 10 leaves using medium Cut-Out. Let flowers and leaves dry on cornstarch-dusted surface. When dry, brush flowers and leaves with water and sprinkle with Shimmer Dust to match colors; let dry. Attach medium daisy to center of large daisy with thinned fondant (p. 101). Roll small white balls of fondant and attach for flower centers with damp brush; let dry. Cut 3 florist wires to 13 in., 3 to 10 in., 2 to 9 in. and 3 to 8 in. When dry, attach flowers and leaves to florist wires with thinned fondant; set aside.

Prepare 3-layer cake (two 2 in. and one 1 in. high to make a 5 in. high cake) for rolled fondant by lightly icing with buttercream. Cover cakes with white fondant (p. 97); smooth with Easy-Glide Smoother. Combine remaining violet fondant from flowers with white fondant to equal 15 oz.; add a small amount of violet icing color for shade used on embossed stripes. Tint 5 oz. white fondant with Royal Blue icing color for shade used

on smooth stripes. Roll out violet fondant $3/16$ in. thick; using Cutter/Embosser with 2 straight-edge cutters and 2 striped embossing wheels (no spacers), cut 8 double-wide strips, 5 in. long. Roll out blue fondant $3/16$ in. thick; using 2 straight-edge cutters and one $1/3$ in. spacer, cut 8 smooth strips, 5 in. long. Attach strips, alternating blue and violet, to cake sides with damp brush. For bottom border, roll $3/4$ in. balls of white fondant and attach to cake with thinned fondant. Pipe swirls on top of balls with white Icing Writer. For top border, roll $5/8$ in. white fondant balls and attach with thinned fondant. Cut dowel rod to height of cake and insert into cake center. Drop a piece of fondant into dowel rod to secure flowers. Position flowers.
Serves 18.

Perfect for These Events:
Mother's Day, female birthday, anniversary, bridal shower

Also Try These Ideas:
For showers, change colors to pastel. For weddings, create a cake centerpiece for each table or dessert station.

Rockin' Wrapping!

Here's a party cake with presence! It's packed with layer upon layer of packages in electric colors and fun shapes like swirls, polka dots and stripes. Proof that when it comes to mixing textures and colors, no icing is more gifted than fondant.

Project Checklist

- **Pans:** 6, 8 x 2 in. Round
- **Tips:** 8, 10
- **Fondant:** White Ready-To-Use Rolled Fondant (96 oz. needed), Primary and Neon Colors Fondant Multi Packs, Square Cut-Outs™, Cutter/Embosser, Brush Set, Perfect Height™ Rolling Pin, Roll & Cut Mat, Easy-Glide Fondant Smoother, p. 114-119
- **Recipe:** Buttercream Icing, p. 101
- **Also:** 8 in. Lollipop Sticks, 12 in. Cake Circles (3 needed), Fanci-Foil Wrap, Piping Gel, Wooden Dowel Rods, cornstarch, small plastic ruler, cellophane tape

In advance: Make 4 fondant gifts on lollipop sticks for top of cake. Combine colors as follows for all gifts used on cake. For light green, add 3 oz. white fondant to 2 oz. primary green; reserve remaining primary green. For blue, add 4 oz. white to 4 oz. blue. For light yellow, add 4 oz. white to 4 oz. neon yellow. For orange, add 4 oz. white to 4 oz. neon orange. For light pink, add 2 oz. white to 2 oz. neon pink; reserve remaining neon pink. For dark purple, add 2 oz. white to 4 oz. purple; divide in half. For light purple, add an additional 2 oz. white to half of the dark purple. Use primary red, primary yellow and reserved primary green and neon pink as is. Roll out fondant $1/8$ in. thick. Cut gifts from $1^1/2$ in. square to 3 x 4 in. high rectangle with straight-edge wheel of Cutter/Embosser. For gift decorations, roll fondant $1/16$ in. thick. Cut strips for ribbons $3/8$ in., $1/4$ in. and $5/16$ in. wide; attach to gifts with damp brush. Cut dots using small openings of tips 8 and 10; attach with damp brush. For swirls, cut strips $1/16$ in. wide and roll into swirl shapes; attach. For bow loops, roll and flatten small balls of fondant; pinch end to form a teardrop shape; attach with damp brush. Roll small balls for knots and attach with damp brush. Cut streamers in same widths as ribbons, trim ends at angles; attach with damp brush. Let all gifts

dry on cornstarch-dusted surface. When completely dry, attach lollipop stick to backs of gifts with thinned fondant; let dry.

For base board, tape three 12 in. cake circles together and cover with fondant (p. 99), smooth with Easy-Glide Smoother. Prepare 2-layer cakes for rolled fondant by lightly icing with buttercream. Prepare 8 in. cake for stacked construction (p. 99). Cover cakes with fondant (p. 97); smooth with Easy-Glide Smoother. For cake sides, cut fondant gifts and decorations in assorted colors using medium and large square Cut-Outs™ or cutting with Cutter/Embosser as for gifts on sticks (about 17 gifts for top cake, 21 for bottom cake). Attach immediately to cake with damp brush, positioning larger gifts in back, smaller gifts in front. Insert gifts on sticks in cake top. **Serves 32.**

Perfect for These Events:
General birthday, holiday, wedding or baby shower

Also Try These Ideas:
Vary package colors to suit the event. Serve as a Christmas centerpiece or a gift table decoration.

Rainbow Skyscraper

Don't be shy about creating new colors with your fondant. You can customize the color by kneading together tinted fondant and adding small amounts of icing color, as seen on the peach and periwinkle tiers here. See our color blending chart on page 103 to find more beautiful combinations.

Project Checklist

- **Pans:** 6, 8, 10, 12, 14 x 2 in. Round

- **Icing Colors:** Creamy Peach, Rose, Violet

- **Fondant:** Ready-To-Use Rolled Fondant in White, Pastel Green (72 oz. each needed), Pastel Pink, Pastel Blue (48 oz. each needed), Pastel Yellow (24 oz. needed), Round Cut-Outs™, Fondant Ribbon Cutter/Embosser Set, Brush Set, Wide Glide™ Rolling Pin, Roll & Cut Mat, Easy-Glide Fondant Smoother, p. 114-119

- **Recipe:** Buttercream Icing, p. 101

- **Also:** Gum-Tex™, p. 119; 16 in. Silver Cake Base, Cake Boards, Dowel Rods, ruler, facial tissue, cornstarch

In advance: Make fondant bow using 24 oz. white fondant with 2 teaspoons of Gum-Tex added for firmness. Roll out fondant $3/16$ in. thick; using 2 beaded embossing wheels with $1/3$ in. spacer, cut 12 to 18 strips, 6 in. long. Make bow loops (p. 108); let dry on cornstarch-dusted surface. For bow base, roll fondant $1/8$ in. thick and cut a 3 in. circle; let dry. Attach loops to base, in overlapping fashion, with thinned fondant. Let dry.

Prepare 2-layer cakes for stacked construction (p. 99). Prepare cakes for rolled fondant by lightly icing with buttercream. Cover 6, 10 and 14 in. cakes with yellow, pink and green fondant respectively (p. 97); smooth with Easy-Glide Smoother. Reserve remaining green, $2^{1}/2$ oz. of yellow fondant, $3^{1}/2$ oz. of pink fondant for ball borders. For peach, combine remaining yellow and pink fondant; if needed, add white fondant to create 24 oz. of this combination. Knead in peach icing color and cover 8 in. cake; smooth. Reserve remaining peach fondant for ball border. For periwinkle, knead rose and violet icing colors

into pastel blue fondant. Cover 12 in. cake and smooth; reserve remaining periwinkle for ball border. Roll out white fondant $1/8$ in. thick and cut about 500 circles using smallest round Cut-Out. Attach circles in vertical rows of 4, spaced $1/2$ in. apart around each cake, using a damp brush. Roll $1/2$ in. diameter balls and attach for bottom borders with damp brush. Position bow on cake top.

Serves 196 (wedding-size servings)* or 163 (party-size servings).

*Note: The top tier is often saved for the first anniversary. The number of servings given does not include top tier.

Perfect for These Events:
Wedding, large baby or wedding shower, Quinceañera

Also Try These Ideas:
Create a white-on-white wedding cake. Adjust size from 1 to 5 tiers depending on your guest list. Reverse the color with white cakes and multli-colored dots. Cut out stars or flowers rather than dots.

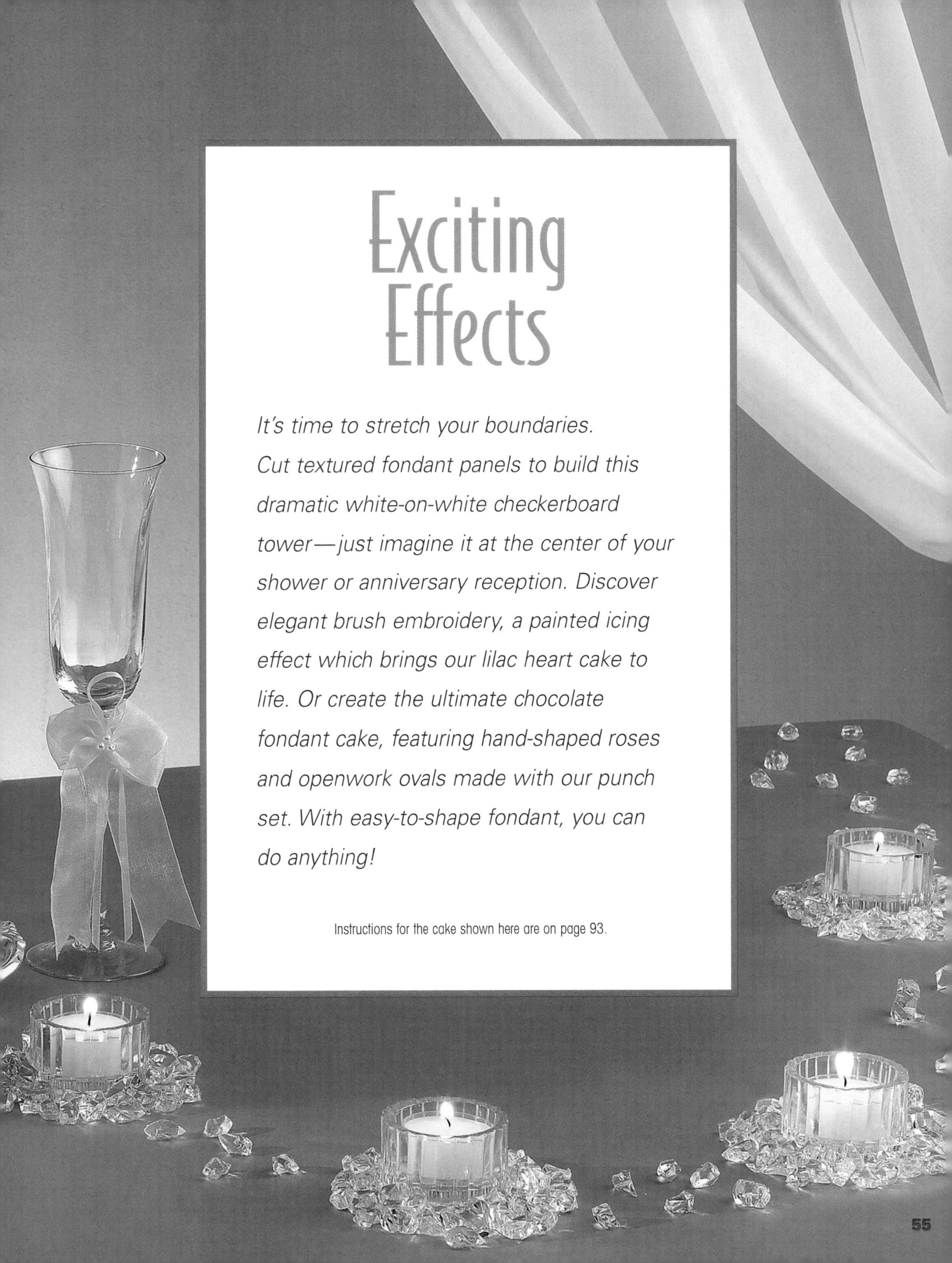

Exciting Effects

*It's time to stretch your boundaries.
Cut textured fondant panels to build this
dramatic white-on-white checkerboard
tower—just imagine it at the center of your
shower or anniversary reception. Discover
elegant brush embroidery, a painted icing
effect which brings our lilac heart cake to
life. Or create the ultimate chocolate
fondant cake, featuring hand-shaped roses
and openwork ovals made with our punch
set. With easy-to-shape fondant, you can
do anything!*

Instructions for the cake shown here are on page 93.

Sweets for the Sweet

Make every guest feel like a kid in a candy store! They'll be tempted to pick off one of the sugar-dusted gumdrops, swirling lollipops or wrapped sour balls—the shaped fondant could fool anyone. Just have them wait until they blow out the candles!

Project Checklist

- **Pans:** 6, 10 x 2 in. Round
- **Tip:** 2
- **Icing Colors:** Golden Yellow, Lemon Yellow
- **Fondant:** White Ready-To-Use Rolled Fondant (96 oz. needed), Fondant Multi Packs in Neon and Primary Colors (2 pks. each needed), Alphabet/Number Cut-Outs™, Brush Set, Perfect Height™ Rolling Pin, Roll & Cut Mat, Easy-Glide Fondant Smoother, p. 114-119
- **Recipe:** Buttercream Icing, p. 101
- **Also:** Gum-Tex™, p. 119; 8 in. Cookie Treat Sticks, Cake Boards, Fanci-Foil Wrap, Cake Dividing Set, cornstarch, granulated sugar

In advance: Make the fondant candies; (make extras to allow for breakage). For 48 spice drops, shape various neon and primary colors of fondant into $3/4$ x $5/8$ in. rounded cones. Brush with water, roll in granulated sugar. For 22 assorted wrapped candies, see instructions below. For 3 lollipops, make multi-colored ropes (p. 108) using 2 primary or neon logs between 1 white log; roll logs 24 x $1/4$ in. diameter. Coil completed rope into a spiral. Insert stick. Let all pieces dry on cornstarch-dusted surface.

Bake and cool 2-layer cakes and prepare for stacked construction (p. 99). Prepare cakes for rolled fondant by lightly icing in buttercream; cover cakes with fondant (p. 97) and smooth with Easy-Glide Fondant Smoother. For cake base, tint 24 oz. of white fondant with Golden Yellow/Lemon Yellow combination; cover 14 in. cake circle with yellow fondant (p. 99). Using Cake Dividing Set, divide 10 in. layer into 10ths and 6 in. layer into 6ths. Assemble cakes on base. For swags, make multi-colored

ropes using 1 white log and one primary or neon log, each $3/8$ in. diameter. Cut into $4 1/4$ in. lengths for 10 in. tier and 4 in. lengths for 6 in. tier. Attach swags between division marks using thinned fondant. Roll a $1/4$ in. diameter white log for each bottom border and attach with damp brush. Attach 3 spice drops at division marks with thinned fondant (p. 101) and tip 2. Add a small amount of Gum-Tex to red fondant, cut message using alphabet Cut-Outs and attach to cakes with damp brush. Position wrapped candies. Insert lollipops into cake top.

Serves 40.

Perfect for These Events:
Kids' birthday, sweet table centerpiece

Also Try These Ideas:
Create other favorite candy shapes or switch to pastel colors. Substitute candles for the lollipops on top.

WRAPPED CANDIES

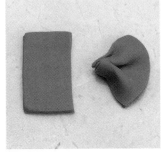

1. Shape neon and primary colors of fondant into 1 in. long x $1/2$ in. high x $5/8$ in. wide rectangles or 1 in. diameter balls with flat bottoms.

2. Roll and cut two $3/4$ x $1 1/2$ in. wrapper strips for each candy. Brush one long edge with water, then form pleat.

3. Cut slits in opposite sides of rectangles and balls and insert pleated ends to attach.

Express Delivery

This construction truck has a unique suspension — a cake board and craft block base that supports its five cakes almost invisibly. Its cargo of fondant gifts and candy will be enjoyed by guys of all ages.

Project Checklist

- **Pan:** 6 x 2 in. Square

- **Icing Colors:** Red-Red, Christmas Red, Black, Lemon Yellow, Golden Yellow

- **Fondant:** White Ready-To-Use Rolled Fondant (72 oz. needed), Primary Colors Fondant Multi Pack, Round and Square Cut-Outs™, Cutter/Embosser, Brush Set, Perfect Height™ Rolling Pin, Roll & Cut Mat, Easy-Glide Fondant Smoother, p. 114-119

- **Recipe:** Buttercream Icing, p. 101

- **Also:** Truck Side Window Pattern, p. 113; Gum-Tex™, p. 119; 101 Cookie Cutters Set, Cake Boards, Fanci-Foil Wrap, round toothpick, paring knife, craft block, hot glue gun, cornstarch, assorted candies

In advance: Make fondant wheels and hubcaps. Add $1^{1}/2$ teaspoons of Gum-Tex to 20 oz. of white fondant. Tint 12 oz. fondant black and 8 oz. gray. Roll out black fondant $^{3}/8$ in. thick and cut 2 front wheels using large round cookie cutter; cut out center of wheels using medium round cookie cutter. Cut 4 back wheels using medium round cookie cutter; cut out centers using small round Cut-Out. Roll out gray fondant and cut 2 front hubcaps using medium round cookie cutter. Insert into large wheel and smooth. Cut 4 back hubcaps using small round Cut-Out; insert into back wheels and smooth. Make spoke impressions on hubcaps with toothpick. Let all fondant pieces dry on cornstarch-dusted surface.

Make packages using primary Multi Pack colors; roll out fondant $^{1}/8$ in. thick and cut using large and medium square Cut-Outs. Cut $^{1}/8$ in. wide strips for ribbon; attach with damp brush. Roll small balls and shape into teardrops for bows; attach. Roll small balls for knots; attach.

Bake and cool five 1-layer 6 in. square cakes (trim each cake to $1^{1}/2$ in. high). Follow instructions below for assembling

truck. Prepare cakes for rolled fondant by lightly icing with buttercream. Tint 24 oz. of fondant red (combine Red-Red and Christmas Red) and 24 oz. yellow (combine Lemon Yellow and Golden Yellow). Cover front cab of truck with red fondant and back payload area with yellow fondant (p. 98). Smooth areas with Easy-Glide Smoother. Roll out white fondant $^{1}/4$ in. thick and cut a $5^{1}/4$ x $2^{1}/4$ in. high piece for front windshield; attach with damp brush. Using pattern, cut two side window pieces (reverse pattern for 2nd window); attach with damp brush. For each window frame, cut four $^{1}/4$ in. wide red strips, cut ends at angles to form frame corners and attach with damp brush. Roll out yellow fondant $^{3}/8$ in. thick and cut a $6^{1}/4$ x 7 in. section to curve over roof and back of cab; attach with damp brush. For lip on cab roof, cut a $^{5}/8$ x $6^{1}/4$ in. strip of yellow fondant; attach. For side trim on payload area, cut 15 yellow strips, $^{1}/2$ x 2 in.; attach with damp brush. For top edges of payload area, cut three $^{1}/2$ x $6^{1}/4$ in. yellow strips; attach with damp brush. Using knife, cut $^{3}/4$ in. yellow circles for front headlights and $^{3}/8$ in. circles for top headlights; attach.

Cut 1 x 19 in. gray fondant strip for bottom of payload area; attach. Cut a $5^{1}/2$ x $2^{1}/4$ in. gray piece for front grille; using straight-edge wheel of Cutter/Embosser, imprint grille lines. Cut three $2^{1}/4$ x $^{1}/2$ in. gray strips for grille front; attach strips and grille with damp brush. For front bumper, roll out gray fondant $^{1}/2$ in. thick and cut a 6 x $^{3}/4$ in. strip; attach. For wheel wells, roll a 1 x 7 in. red log; cut lengthwise in half and attach, flattening and trimming end for running board.

Attach wheels to truck with damp brush. Position gift packages and candies in truck.

Serves 30.

Perfect for These Events:
Any age boys' birthday, truck driver or construction worker birthday, construction company party

Also Try These Ideas:
Add the name, event or date. Fill the back with additional candy if you want to skip the gifts.

ASSEMBLING THE TRUCK

1. To make base, cut three 2 x 2 x 5 in. pieces of craft block. Wrap craft blocks and 6 x 12 in. double cake board with foil. Glue craft blocks in place at wheel areas of truck on bottom of cake board.

2. Fill and stack four square cakes and position on craft blocks. Cut the other cake in half; fill and stack halves. Trim cut side at a slight angle. Position for front cab of truck.

3. Decorate assembled cake following instructions above.

Sweet Wishes

The chocolate fondant roses are incredible—but look closely at the lovely inlay and openwork designs made with our Decorative Punch Set. They let the ivory fondant peek through to lighten the look.

Project Checklist

- **Pans:** Oval Set ($10^3/4$ x $7^5/8$ in. and $16^1/2$ x $12^3/8$ in. used)

- **Tips:** 3, 6

- **Icing Colors:** Brown, Red-Red, Ivory

- **Fondant:** White Ready-To-Use Rolled Fondant (126 oz. needed), Oval Cut-Outs™, 9-Pc. Fondant Decorative Punch Set, Brush Set, Wide Glide™ Rolling Pin, Roll & Cut Mat, Easy-Glide Fondant Smoother, p. 114-119

- **Recipes:** Chocolate Fondant (5 batches needed), Buttercream Icing, p. 101

- **Also:** Stepsaving Rose Bouquets Flower Cutter Set, Confectionery Tool Set, p. 119; Cake Boards, Fanci-Foil Wrap, Dowel Rods, toothpicks, vegetable shortening, 6 x 12 x 1 in. high craft block, large base board or serving plate

In advance: Make chocolate fondant roses and leaves. Reserve 6 oz. of white fondant and tint ivory; set aside. Prepare 5 recipes of chocolate fondant. Add Brown and Red-Red icing color to chocolate fondant to achieve a deeper color. Follow instructions in flower cutter set to make four full-bloom roses using large cutter, three 2-layer roses using large cutter, three full-bloom roses using small cutter, two 2-layer roses using small cutter and one rosebud using large cutter, plus 12 leaves. Make roses on toothpicks lightly coated with vegetable shortening. Insert in craft block to dry. Use veining tool from confectionery set to imprint veins in leaves. Let dry. Reserve remaining fondant.

Prepare 2-layer $10^3/4$ x $7^5/8$ in. and 1-layer $16^1/2$ x $12^3/8$ in. oval cakes for stacked construction (p. 99). Prepare cakes for rolled fondant by lightly icing with buttercream. Cover both cakes with chocolate fondant rolled $1/8$ in. thick (p. 97); smooth with Easy-Glide Smoother. Using 4-Leaf Clover Punch, punch out designs 1 in. apart around top edge of bottom cake. If needed, lift out punched portion with a toothpick. Roll out ivory fondant $1/8$ in. thick and punch out same design; insert ivory designs in punched out areas on cake, smooth gently. For top cake, roll out

additional chocolate fondant $1/8$ in. thick; using Dutch Blossom Punch, punch out design. Center large oval Cut-Out around design area and cut out oval. Repeat for a total of 8 ovals. Roll out ivory fondant $1/8$ in. thick and cut 8 large ovals. Attach ivory ovals, topped by chocolate ovals, $1^1/2$ in. apart on cake sides with damp brush. Using thinned fondant (p. 101), pipe tip 6 beads* around each oval. Using smallest Cut-Out, cut 8 chocolate ovals; attach between large ovals with damp brush. Position cakes; pipe tip 6 bead bottom borders on cakes with thinned fondant. Remove toothpicks from roses and attach roses and leaves to cake top with tip 6 and thinned fondant. Write tip 3 message with thinned fondant.*
Serves 42.

***Note:** For instructions on specific piping techniques, see the Wilton Yearbook of Cake Decorating or visit www.wilton.com.

Perfect for These Events:
Retirement, anniversary, male birthday, graduation

Also Try These Ideas:
Create a white fondant cake with multi-color roses and insets. Change the cake shape to hearts or rounds.

Honor Roll Scroll

How do you make brown bold? Tint fondant in several shades and roll them together in this sophisticated striped treatment. It's a great backdrop for the lively fondant curls.

Project Checklist

- **Pans:** Hexagon Set (9 x 2, 15 x 2 in. used)
- **Icing Colors:** Brown, Red-Red
- **Fondant:** White Ready-To-Use Rolled Fondant (160 oz. needed), Cutter/Embosser, Brush Set, Wide Glide™ Rolling Pin, Roll & Cut Mat, Easy-Glide Fondant Smoother, p. 114-119
- **Recipe:** Buttercream Icing, p. 101
- **Also:** Graduation Cap and Scroll Patterns, p. 112; Confectionery Tool Set, Gum-Tex™, p. 118-119; Piping Gel, Plastic Dowel Rods, 8 in. Lollipop Sticks, White Candy Melts®* (1 pk. needed), Fanci-Foil Wrap, ruler, cornstarch, triple-thick sturdy cardboard, toothpick

In advance: Make fondant cap, scroll and curls. For cap, tint 16 oz. fondant dark brown combined with a little red-red. Roll out ⅛ in. thick, trace pattern with toothpick and cut out. For scroll, roll out white fondant ⅛ in. thick, trace pattern and cut out. Cut a ¾ in. wide dark brown strip for ribbon and attach with damp brush. Using veiner tool from Confectionery Tool Set, score line on cap and folds on scroll. For tassel, tint 2 oz. fondant light brown and make a ⅛ x 2 in. long rope (p. 108). For fringe, cut a 1 x 1½ in. rectangle, then cut thin slits, stopping ⅛ in. from edge. Wrap fringe around rope. Attach to cap with damp brush. For button, roll a ¼ in. dark brown ball; flatten and attach with damp brush. Reserve all leftover dark brown fondant for cake stripes and board. Let cap and scroll dry on cornstarch-dusted board. When dry, attach lollipop stick to back with melted candy, leave 3 in. at bottom to insert in cake. Let set. To make approximately 72 curls (see below), add 3 teaspoons of Gum-Tex to 48 oz. of white fondant; knead well.

Prepare 2-layer cakes for stacked construction (p. 99); prepare for rolled fondant by lightly icing with buttercream. Cover cakes with fondant (p. 98); smooth with Easy-Glide Smoother. For striped side panels, make colors as follows: for light brown, combine a 1 in. ball of dark brown with 10 oz. of white fondant;

for medium brown, combine a 1½ in. ball of dark brown with 8 oz. of white fondant. Follow striping process (p. 102), cutting panels to match hexagon side measurements, and alternating ⅛ in. wide dark brown strips with ¼ in. wide medium and light brown strips. Attach to cake with damp brush, trimming to fit as needed and using Smoother to blend seams. Use excess fondant to make additional colored fondant if needed.

Cut a triple-thick cake board to accommodate cake with a bottom layer of curls. Add white fondant to reserved brown fondant to make approximately 48 oz. of medium brown. Cover prepared board with fondant (p. 99); smooth with Easy-Glide Smoother. Position cakes; attach curls with melted candy. Insert cap and position scroll.
Serves 68.

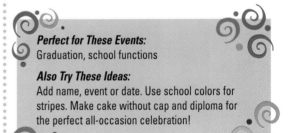

Perfect for These Events:
Graduation, school functions

Also Try These Ideas:
Add name, event or date. Use school colors for stripes. Make cake without cap and diploma for the perfect all-occasion celebration!

CURLS

1. Roll out fondant ⅛ in. thick and cut approximately 72 strips, 1 x 7 in.

2. Roll strips in loose curls, leaving flat surfaces open and giving some longer uncurled tails. Let dry on side, on cornstarch-dusted board.

3. Curls will be attached to cake and board with melted candy.

A Planter's Paradise

The multi-colored flowers show a touch of fantasy while the potting equipment couldn't look more real! This is why working with fondant is so satisfying—you have the versatility to create the natural folds of a glove or go wild with any blossom design you can imagine.

Project Checklist

- **Pan:** Petal Pan Set (15 in. used), Mini Wonder Mold, Cookie Sheets

- **Icing Colors:** Violet, Rose, Lemon Yellow, Terra Cotta, Brown, Black, Kelly Green

- **Fondant:** Ready-to-Use Rolled Fondant in Pastel Blue (72 oz. needed), White and Pastel Green (48 oz. each needed), Cut-Outs™ in Flower, Daisy and Leaf shapes, Icing Writer™ in Pink, Violet and Yellow, FoodWriters™ in Bold Tip and Fine Tip Primary Colors and Fine Tip Neon Colors, Brush Set, Perfect Height™ Rolling Pin, Roll & Cut Mat, Easy-Glide Fondant Smoother, p. 114-119

- **Recipe:** Buttercream Icing, p. 101

- **Also:** Picket Fence and Trowel Patterns, p. 113; Flower Former Set, Gum-Tex™, p. 118-119; Cake Boards, Fanci-Foil Wrap, Plastic Dowel Rods, ruler, craft knife, embroidery scissors, 18 gauge cloth-covered florist wire (three each 10 in. and 8 in., one each 7 in. and 5 in.), chocolate cookie crumbs, cornstarch

At least 3-4 days in advance: Make fondant flowers, leaves, trowel, seed packet, gloves, fence pickets and posts. Add 2 teaspoons Gum-Tex to 24 oz. white fondant. For flowers, tint 3 in. balls of white fondant light rose, violet and yellow; knead in $1/2$ teaspoon additional Gum-Tex to each. Roll out colors $1/8$ in. thick and cut flowers for flower pot: 2 pink and 1 yellow using large flower Cut-Out, 3 violet and 1 yellow using medium daisy Cut-Out, 1 violet and 1 yellow using large daisy Cut-Out and 1 violet using medium flower Cut-Out. Attach 1 medium daisy to each large daisy with damp brush. Using small flower and daisy Cut-Outs, cut various color small blossoms. Tint a 2 in. ball of green fondant, add $1/2$ teaspoon Gum-Tex, roll out $1/8$ in. thick and cut 6 leaves using medium Cut-Out. Let all flowers and leaves dry on cornstarch-dusted surface. When dry, roll $1/8$ in. balls of white fondant for flower centers and attach with damp brush. Using Icing Writer, pipe lines on flowers. Using Bold Tip green FoodWriter, draw veins. Attach flowers and leaves to wires with thinned fondant (p. 101); let dry.

For 36 pickets, roll out 24 oz. of white fondant $1/8$ in. thick and cut using pattern. For fence posts, roll out white fondant $3/8$ in. thick and cut $3/8$ x $2^1/2$ in. long strips. For post tops, roll 8 balls, $3/8$ in. diameter. Let all dry. For trowel, tint a $1^1/2$ in. ball of white fondant gray using black icing color; knead in $1/2$ teaspoon additional Gum-Tex; using pattern, cut trowel. Let dry on flower former dusted with cornstarch. For seed packet, cut a $2^1/2$ x $3^1/2$ in. strip of white and a $2^1/4$ x 2 in. strip of green. Attach green strip to white with damp brush. Attach various color small blossoms with damp brush. With Fine Tip green FoodWriter, draw stems and leaves, print "SEEDS". Let dry with corner against flower former. For gloves, roll out white fondant $1/4$ in. thick. Use toothpick to carefully trace around your hands. Cut out hands with craft knife, starting $1/4$ in. inside tracing for smaller gloves. Gently smooth edges, fold thumbs under and slightly bend areas for a soft look. Cut a strip the length of wrist area, $1/2$ in. wide; attach under wrist for dimension using a damp brush. Attach small blossoms with damp brush; using FoodWriters, add purple dot flower centers and pink decorative dots to gloves. Let dry.

Also in advance: Make cake base. Cut three 18 in. cake boards $1^1/2$ in. wider than 15 in. petal pan. Cover prepared board with 36 oz. of pastel green fondant (p. 99) and smooth with Easy-Glide Smoother. Let dry.

Prepare 2-layer 15 in. petal cake (3 in. high) for rolled fondant by lightly icing with buttercream. Cover with pastel blue fondant; smooth with Easy-Glide Smoother. Position on cake base. Attach 4 pickets to each petal division with damp brush; attach posts and tops at division points with damp brush. For grass, tint remaining pastel green fondant with Leaf Green icing color. Roll out $1/8$ in. thick and cut $1/2$ x 3 in. long strips. Cut fringe on one edge with scissors and attach at bottom border with damp brush. Add more layers, tucking between first layers. Attach small blossoms with damp brush. For trowel handle, roll a $3^3/4$ x $1/2$ in. wide log of dark green fondant; cut a notch in one end with scissors. Using rounded end of brush, make a hanging hole at top of handle. Insert trowel in handle.

Tint 16 oz. white fondant terra cotta mixed with a little brown. Prepare Mini Wonder Mold cake for rolled fondant by lightly icing with buttercream. Cover cake with terra cotta fondant; smooth. Turn cake wide side up. Roll out terra cotta $5/16$ in. thick and cut a $1^3/4$ in. strip to wrap around top edge of cake; attach with damp brush, extending $1/4$ in. higher than cake edge. For flowerpot tray, cut a $3^1/2$ in. cake board circle. Roll terra cotta fondant $1/4$ in. thick and cut a $3^1/2$ in. circle; place on board. Cut a $3/4$ in. wide strip to wrap around circle; attach. Cut a $3/8$ in. wide strip to overlap previous strip; attach. Cut a $1/4$ in. wide strip and attach to cover seam along top edge. Position flower pot cake on tray. Insert a plastic dowel rod cut to height of pot, in center of cake; remove cake inside rod and position rod. Place a piece of fondant at bottom of rod to secure flowers. Position flowers, then position flower pot on petal cake. Sprinkle top of flower pot with cookie crumbs. Position trowel, seed packet and gloves.

Serves 30.

Perfect for These Events:
Female birthday, Mother's Day, garden party

Also Try These Ideas:
Vary flower shapes and colors. Give real seed packets and garden tools as favors.

Cover All the Bases

Talk about non-stop action! Every ball is in play as individual cut-outs are trimmed and positioned like puzzle pieces using the easy inlay technique. It's the perfect cake for any sports fan who loves when all the seasons overlap.

Project Checklist

- **Pans:** 10 x 2 in. Round

- **Icing Colors:** Brown, Red-Red, Orange, White-White

- **Fondant:** White Ready-To-Use Rolled Fondant (60 oz. needed), Bold Tip Primary FoodWriters™, Brush Set, Perfect Height™ Rolling Pin, Roll & Cut Mat, Easy-Glide Fondant Smoother, p. 114-119

- **Recipe:** Buttercream Icing, p. 101

- **Also:** Soccer Ball Pattern, p. 113; 101 Cookie Cutters Set, Cake Circle, Fanci-Foil Wrap, cornstarch, toothpicks, craft knife

Prepare 2-layer cake for rolled fondant by lightly icing with buttercream. Cover cake with 36 oz. of white fondant; smooth with Easy-Glide Smoother. Tint 6 oz. fondant brown/red-red combination for footballs. Tint 6 oz. fondant orange/brown combination for basketballs. Reserve 12 oz. white for soccer balls and baseballs. On mat dusted with cornstarch, roll out each color $1/8$ in. thick. Cut one basketball, soccer ball and baseball using medium round cutter and one football using football cutter. Follow inlay directions below for cutting and positioning on cake. Repeat procedure, cutting more ball groups to cover entire cake. Let set for 2 to 4 hours. Trace soccer ball seam pattern. Draw detail on basketballs, baseballs and soccer balls with FoodWriters. Paint stitching and seams on footballs using brush and white-white icing color.
Serves 28.

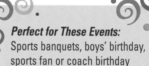

Perfect for These Events:
Sports banquets, boys' birthday, sports fan or coach birthday

Also Try These Ideas:
Serve ball cookies topped with the same fondant ball decorations which top the cake—all cut with the 101 Cutters Set.

INLAYS

1. On fondant-covered cake, position a cut ball.

2. Position other balls on cake to determine overlapping areas. Mark overlaps with a toothpick. Remove from cake and use cutters to trim off overlapping portions so that balls fit neatly together.

3. Attach each ball grouping with damp brush. Smooth with Easy-Glide Smoother.

A Budding Romance

Brush embroidery blossoms help this cake achieve a perfectly balanced look. Because the petals and leaves are painted flat against the surface, you can clearly see the pretty heart-shaped cakes, the graceful rope border and the flowing sculptured ornament.

Project Checklist

- **Pans:** 8, 14 x 2 in. Heart

- **Tips:** 1, 2

- **Icing Colors*:** Violet, Rose, Lemon Yellow, Golden Yellow, Moss Green, Kelly Green

- **Fondant:** Ready-To-Use Rolled Fondant in White (96 oz. needed) and Pastel Blue (24 oz. needed), Flower and Leaf Cut-Outs™, Brush Set, Wide Glide™ Rolling Pin, Roll & Cut Mat, Easy-Glide Fondant Smoother, p. 114-119

- **Recipes:** Buttercream Icing, Royal Icing, p. 101

- **Also:** Bianca Figurine, Cake Boards, Fanci-Foil Wrap, Piping Gel, Meringue Powder, Wooden Dowel Rods, craft knife

In advance: Prepare base board. Cut three cake boards 1 in. wider than 14 in. heart pan; tape together. Cover prepared board with 24 oz. of white fondant (p. 99) and smooth with Easy-Glide Smoother.

Prepare 2-layer heart cakes (3 in. high) for stacked construction. Prepare cakes for rolled fondant by lightly icing with buttercream. Combine 72 oz. of white fondant with 24 oz. of pastel blue fondant, then knead in a small amount of violet icing color. Cover cakes with fondant (p. 98); smooth with Easy-Glide Smoother.

Position cakes on base board. Imprint cakes with medium flower and small leaf Cut-Outs, in cascading fashion, on opposite sides. For areas which overhang cake edges, imprint top portion of Cut-Out, then line up bottom portion and imprint on cake side. Using thinned royal icing and tip 2, outline flowers and leaves one at a time and immediately brush for brush embroidery (see p. 105). Using full-strength royal icing, pipe tip 2 dot[†] flower centers and tip 1 vines[†]. Roll a rope (p. 108), for each bottom border; attach with damp brush. Position figurine on cake board cut to fit.

Serves 72 (wedding-size servings) ** **or 66 (party-size servings).**

***Note:** Combine Violet and Rose for flower shade shown; combine Kelly Green and Moss Green for leaf and vine shade shown; combine Golden Yellow and Lemon Yellow for flower centers shade shown.

[†]**Note:** For instructions on specific piping techniques, see the Wilton Yearbook of Cake Decorating or visit www.wilton.com.

****Note:** The top tier is often saved for the first anniversary. The number of servings given does not include the top tier.

Perfect for These Events:
Wedding, anniversary, bridal shower, birthday, Valentine's Day

Also Try These Ideas:
Change the color scheme, try pink or lavender. Add tiers for more servings or make one tier for a more intimate gathering.

Best Kid on the Block!

Small cakes grow tall: The little square tiers stand out thanks to a variety of pretty fondant colors and fun cut-out shapes. They stand up because they're built on the sturdy Tall Tier Cake Stand with a center column support.

Project Checklist

- **Pans:** 6 x 2 in. Square (2 pans needed)

- **Fondant:** Ready-To-Use Rolled Fondant in White (288 oz. needed), Pastel Pink and Pastel Blue (96 oz. each needed), Pastel Yellow and Pastel Green (48 oz. each needed), Brush Set, Perfect Height™ Rolling Pin, Roll & Cut Mat, Easy-Glide Fondant Smoother, p. 114-119

- **Recipe:** Buttercream Icing, p. 101

- **Also:** #1 Numeral Candle, Flowerful Medley Sprinkle Decorations, Tall Tier Cake Stand Basic Set components, including 18 in. Separator Plate (footed), 6¹/2 in. Columns (4 needed), Top Column Cap Nut and Bottom Column Bolt, Cake Corer Tube, Plastic Dowel Rods (2 pks. needed), 14 in. & 16 in. Cake Circles (one of each), Cake Boards (16 cut into 6 in. squares), A-B-C and 1-2-3 (50-Pc.) Cutter Set, 101 Cookie Cutters Set, Fanci-Foil Wrap, Piping Gel, 22 in. round triple-thick cardboard, vegetable shortening, balloons, plastic ruler, waxed paper, cornstarch

In advance: Prepare base board. Using cake corer as a guide, cut a hole in the center of 22 in. triple-thick cardboard. Knead together 48 oz. each of Pastel Pink and Pastel Blue fondant to make violet. Cover prepared board with fondant (p. 99) and smooth with Easy-Glide Smoother. Reserve remaining violet fondant. Roll out fondant colors ¹/16 in. thick. Using violet fondant and alphabet cutters, cut 1 set of B-A-B-Y letters. Use shaped cookie cutters to cut 7 stars, ducks, hearts and trains in assorted colors. Let all pieces dry on cornstarch-dusted board.

Prepare 8 cake boards for stacked cakes. Using cake corer, mark center of boards and cut out. Tape 2 boards together and wrap with foil. Prepare 8 solid boards for base cakes; tape 2 boards together and wrap with foil. Prepare eight 3-layer 6 in. cakes (two 2 in. and one 1 in. high to make 5 in. high cakes) for rolled fondant by lightly icing with buttercream. Cover with white fondant (approximately 30 oz. for each cake); smooth with Easy-Glide

Smoother (p. 98). Using cake corer, cut center hole in 3 cakes. Insert dowel rods at corners of 4 base cakes where stacked cakes will rest. Roll out fondant colors ¹/16 in. thick. For each cake side, cut four ³/4 x 6 in. long strips for borders. Trim to fit and attach with damp brush. Attach letters and cut-out designs with damp brush.

At reception, assemble cake (see instructions below). Position confetti sprinkle decorations, candle and balloons.
Serves 96.

Perfect for These Events:
First birthday, baby shower

Also Try These Ideas:
Add more blocks around the cake for larger group. Vary color by using primary colors for blocks.

ASSEMBLING THE BLOCKS

1. Mark center of 14 and 16 in. cake circles using cake corer as a guide. Cut out centers. Level top of 18 in. footed plate by placing 14 in., then 16 in. circles on top center of plate. Position prepared violet base board on top of 16 in. cake circle. Screw in bottom column bolt and one 6¹/2 in. column; position 4 cakes (without center holes) around column.

2. Add 3 additional columns and cakes.

3. Screw on top column cap nut and position top cake over cap.

A Regal Reception

These swirling fondant garlands create the same graceful curves you get from string garlands piped in buttercream. But think of the time they save! With fondant, just roll out, cut the strips and twist.

Project Checklist

- **Pans:** 6, 10, 14 x 2 in. Round

- **Fondant:** White Ready-To-Use Rolled Fondant (576 oz. needed), Cutter/Embosser, Brush Set, Wide Glide™ Rolling Pin, Roll & Cut Mat, Easy-Glide Fondant Smoother, p. 114-119

- **Recipe:** Buttercream Icing, p. 101

- **Also:** Gum-Tex™, p. 119; 12 in. Round Silver Cake Bases (7 needed), Cake Boards, Wooden Dowel Rods, Cake Dividing Set, 10¼ in. Roman Columns (4 needed), 16 in. Decorator Preferred® Separator Plates (2 needed), ruler, silk flowers

Prepare 2-layer cakes (eight 6 in., eight 10 in. and one 14 in.) for Stacked Construction (p. 99). Prepare cakes for rolled fondant by lightly icing with buttercream. Cover cakes with fondant (p. 97) and smooth with Easy-Glide Smoother. For 7 satellite cakes, stack a 6 in. and a 10 in. cake on a silver cake base. For center cake, stack remaining 6, 10 and 14 in. cakes on 16 in. separator plate.

Add 5 teaspoons of Gum-Tex to 60 oz. of fondant to be used for ribbon garlands, bottom borders and balls. Divide 6 in. cakes in 6ths, 10 in. cakes in 10ths and 14 in. cake in 12ths. Follow ribbon garland instructions below; attach ribbons to cake sides with damp brush. Position top garland 1 in. deep, bottom garland 2 in. deep. Roll ¹/₂ in. diameter balls of fondant and attach at each division point with damp brush. For bottom borders, cut ¹/₂ in. wide strips of fondant, ¹/₈ in. thick. Loosely fold segments of strips and attach around bottom borders with damp brush. Finish assembly and position silk flowers at the party. **Serves 466*.**

*Note: The top tier is often saved for the first anniversary. The number of servings given does not include one top tier.

Perfect for These Events: Wedding, anniversary

Also Try These Ideas: Make single cake for smaller events—bridal shower, smaller anniversary party, birthday. Change the look by making pastel garlands and/or pastel covered cakes.

RIBBON GARLANDS

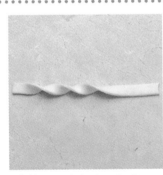

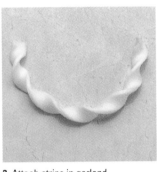

1. Roll out fondant ¹/₁₆ in. thick. Working one strip at a time, cut two ¹/₂ in. wide strips for each cake division in the following lengths. For 6 in. cakes: 5 in. long for top ribbon, 6¹/₂ in. long for bottom ribbon. For 10 in. and 14 in. cakes: 5¹/₂ in. long for top ribbon, 6¹/₂ in. long for bottom ribbon.

2. Hold one end of strip and twist at other end.

3. Attach strips in garland formation with damp brush.

Spectacular Statements

You'll know you're a fondant pro when you can create a masterpiece like this! Look at all the elements working together— from the embossed diamond backdrop in soft green to the curving rose bouquet on top, it's a perfect expression of fondant's versatility. In this section, you'll also find wonderful hand-shaped fondant figures to add personality to your cakes. You'll love making adorable cake toppers like tea party dolls, napping newborns and crazy clowns that make everyone smile!

Instructions for the cake shown here are on page 95.

Picnic Crashers

With fondant, you don't have to sweat the small stuff. Fondant is made for shaping by hand—which means making intricate details is easier than with any other icing. You can roll tiny watermelon seeds, shape the perfect lemonade pitcher or add a squiggle of mustard and have fun doing it all.

Project Checklist

- **Pan:** 9 x 13 x 2 in. Sheet
- **Tips:** 1, 2
- **Icing Colors:** Black, Kelly Green
- **Fondant:** White Ready-To-Use Rolled Fondant (96 oz. needed), Fondant Multi Packs in Primary and Neon (1 pk. each needed) and Natural Colors (2 pks. needed), Square Cut-Outs™, Cutter/Embosser, Brush Set,

Brush-On Color™ in Yellow and Red, Color Tray, Wide Glide™ Rolling Pin, Roll & Cut Mat, Easy-Glide Fondant Smoother, p. 114-119

- **Recipe:** Buttercream Icing, p. 101
- **Also:** Confectionery Tool Set, p. 118; Gum-Tex™, p. 119; 10 x 14 in. Cake Boards (3 needed), Fanci-Foil Wrap, 101 Cookie Cutters Set, Piping Gel, Hidden Pillars, cornstarch, scissors, small knife, 16 x 18 in. cardboard, hot glue gun

Several days in advance: Make the following fondant pieces. For bench seats, mix 1 pk. light brown and 1 pk. dark brown fondant; add ¹/₂ teaspoon of Gum-Tex and knead together. Roll out fondant ¹/₈ in. thick and cut two 13 x 1¹/₂ in. wide strips. Let dry on cornstarch-dusted surface. For hamburger bun tops and bottoms, roll a ³/₄ in. ball of light brown fondant for each and flatten to a 1³/₈ in. circle; make 8. For hamburgers, roll a 1 in. ball of dark-brown fondant for each and flatten to a 1³/₈ in. circle; make 4. Place each hamburger between 2 buns. For hot dog buns, roll a 1 in. ball of light brown fondant into a 2¹/₄ in. oval; cut a center slit with knife; make 3. For hot dogs, roll 1 in. ball of red fondant into a 1³/₄ in. log, make 3. Press into center of bun. For mustard, roll thin strips of yellow fondant and attach to tops of hot dogs with damp brush. For ketchup and mustard bottles, separately roll red and yellow fondant into 1¹/₂ x ³/₄ in. wide logs; flatten ends. Make a ³/₄ in. teardrop in each color for bottle caps and attach with damp brush. For glasses, roll ¹/₂ in. ball of white fondant into a 1 in. log, flatten bottom; make 4. Using medium ball tool from confectionery set, indent inside log for opening. Paint sides with yellow Brush-On Color. For pitcher, roll 2 in. ball of white fondant and shape into a 1¹/₂ in. pitcher. Shape a spout with fingers. Using medium ball tool, indent inside of pitcher for opening. For handle, roll a thin log of white fondant 1¹/₂ in. long and attach with damp brush. Paint sides with yellow Brush-On Color.

For watermelon, roll 1 in. red fondant ball into a 2 x 1¹/₄ in. deep wedge. Roll a 4 x ⁵/₈ in. wide strip of green fondant for rind and attach with damp brush. Roll small black fondant dots and attach for seeds. Repeat process for small watermelon wedges, to measure 1 in. wide at bottom. For plates, roll out white fondant ¹/₈ in. thick; cut 4 plates using medium round cookie cutter and one platter using large round cookie cutter. Mark indentations at plate edges using Cutter/Embosser. Let dry on

cornstarch-dusted surface. For bench and table legs, cut 10 hidden pillars 2 in. long. Mix equal amounts of dark and light brown fondant and attach with damp brush. For grass, tint 48 oz. of white fondant Kelly Green. Roll out ¹/₈ in. thick and cut a 1 x 6 in. strip for each leg; reserve remaining green fondant. Cut slits with scissors for grass blades and attach to bottoms of bench and table legs with damp brush; let dry. For grass board, cut edges of 16 x 18 in. cardboard in a wavy shape using scissors. Roll out reserved green fondant ¹/₈ in. thick. Cover prepared board with fondant (p. 99); smooth with Easy-Glide Smoother.

Prepare 1-layer cake for rolled fondant by lightly icing with buttercream. Cut two 10 x 14 in. cake boards ¹/₂ in. larger than cake, tape together and wrap with foil. Position cake. Roll out white fondant 13 x 17 x ¹/₈ in. thick and position on cake for tablecloth, smoothing top with Easy-Glide Smoother and letting sides fall naturally. Use smallest square Cut-Out to imprint checkerboard pattern on tablecloth beginning at bottom of longest side. Paint alternating squares with red Brush-On Color. Let dry.

Cut an additional board the same size as cake board; wrap with foil. Attach 6 legs (1 in each corner and 2 in center) to bottom of board with hot glue; let dry. Position cake on base at event. Position 2 legs and 1 bench at each table side. In buttercream, pipe tip 2 dot ants with tip 1 pull-out legs. Position dinnerware and food.
Serves 15.

Perfect for These Events:
Picnic, July 4th, BBQ birthday party, Father's Day, office party

Also Try These Ideas:
Substitute other shapes such as fruit, sandwiches, soda bottles. Add a birthday message with Cut-Outs. Decorate a round cake table.

Raising a Ruckus!

It takes a little skill to shape these clowns just right between the bottom cake and the tilted board above. The secret to success—build a mock-up construction using pillars and a craft block, so you can add fondant to the arms if needed.

Project Checklist

- **Pans:** 6, 14 x 2 in. Round
- **Icing Colors:** Orange, Royal Blue, Christmas Red, Red-Red, Kelly Green, Lemon Yellow, Copper (skintone), Rose
- **Fondant:** Ready-To-Use Rolled Fondant in White (192 oz. needed) and Pastel Yellow (24 oz. needed), Brush-On Color™ in Yellow, Orange, Blue and Green, Geometric Cake Stamps™, Bold Tip Primary Colors FoodWriter™, Color Tray, Brush Set, Wide Glide™ Rolling Pin, Roll & Cut Mat, Easy-Glide Fondant Smoother, p. 114-119
- **Recipe:** Buttercream Icing, p. 101
- **Also:** Feet Pattern, p. 112; Gum-Tex™, p. 119; 18 in. Round Silver Cake Base, Cake Circles, Fanci-Foil Wrap, Piping Gel, Tapered Spatula, 101 Cookie Cutters Set, #1 Numeral Candle, Cake Dividing Set, Wooden Dowel Rods, 6 in. Plate and 9 in. Twist Legs from Crystal-Clear Cake Divider Set (plate and legs sold separately), 8 in. Lollipop Sticks, paring knife, craft knife, ruler, scissors, 10 x 10 x 4 in. high craft block, toothpick, waxed paper

At least 1 week in advance: Make 3 fondant clowns following instructions below. Knead in 2 tablespoons Gum-Tex to 36 oz. of white fondant and tint 10 oz. orange, 6 oz. each yellow, green and red-red/Christmas red combination, 4 oz. each blue and copper. After making clowns, reserve leftover fondant.

In advance: Prepare base boards. For top cake, cut a 7 in. diameter cake circle. Wrap with foil. For bottom cake, use 18 in. silver cake base. Cover prepared top board with 8 oz. and bottom board with 36 oz. of white fondant (p. 99) and smooth with Easy-Glide Smoother.

Prepare 2-layer cakes for rolled fondant by lightly icing with buttercream. Cover top cake with yellow, bottom cake with white fondant; smooth with Easy-Glide Smoother. Position cakes on base boards. Using round stamp and Brush-On Color, stamp balloons on bottom cake. Paint streamers using round tip brush; let dry. Tint 6 oz. of white fondant in Red-Red/Christmas Red combination; roll out 1/8 in. thick and cut letters using cookie cutters. Attach with damp brush. Tint 24 oz. fondant blue; make ruffle bottom border (p. 109) and attach with damp brush. Using cake divider, divide 6 in. cake in 6ths. Using remaining blue fondant, roll 3/4 in. balls for bottom border of 6 in. cake and attach. Roll out 8 oz. of white fondant 1/8 in. thick and cut an 8 in. circle. Trim edges of circle in uneven scallops to create icing effect and position circle on cake top. Using 3 oz. of orange fondant, rolled 1/8 in. thick, cut 6 strips, 1/2 x 5 in., for ribbon garland. Twist strips and attach to cake sides with damp brush starting 1 in. from top and draping to 2 in. from top. Roll six 1/2 in. diameter red balls, and attach at garland points with damp brush.

At reception, insert pillars in bottom cake as on mock-up. Position plate and top cake. Position clowns and insert heads, adjusting angle as needed to conform to top cake. Attach hands with thinned fondant (p. 101), adding extra fondant if needed to help hands reach plate. Roll a 1 1/2 in. diameter yellow ball; flatten and insert candle. Position on cake top.
Serves 75.

Perfect for These Events:
1st birthday, kids' birthday

Also Try These Ideas:
Make a 3-tier cake for even more fun. Shape accent clowns in different colors for cake sides.

3-D CLOWNS

1. Make body parts for each clown. Roll a 1 3/8 in. ball of copper fondant for head and a 1/4 in. ball, slightly flattened, for neck. Cut a lollipop stick to 2 1/2 in., brush 1 in. on end with water and insert 1 in. into neck and head. Using 5 1/2 oz. of yellow, green or orange, form a teardrop-shaped body. Slice off tip to flatten top; insert head. For arms, roll two 1/2 x 2 in. long logs in the same color as body. Cut a lollipop stick in 6 1/4 in. and 4 1/4 in. lengths; insert in arms so that 1/4 in. extends at top. For hands, roll 7/8 in. balls and flatten. Using craft knife, cut out a notch for thumb. For hat, cut a 3 1/2 in. diameter fondant circle; cut in half and roll one end toward the other to form a hollow cone, 1 3/4 in. high. Attach edges with damp brush; smooth seams with fingers. On orange hat, cut a 1/8 in. wide strip and attach to base of hat with damp brush. Trace feet pattern on cake board and cut out one for each clown.

2. Cut a wedge from center of body to form legs; bend green clown's legs. Insert arms into body, using longer stick for clown's right arm and pushing diagonally through left leg; longer stick should extend at top and bottom, shorter stick at top only. Cut slits in hands for fingers. Cover feet with fondant, rounding each end to form 2 large shoes. Make a mock-up construction to test positioning of clowns. Insert twist pillars in craft block, then cover top of block with waxed paper. Attach a small amount of fondant to right side pillars, so that they extend 5 1/4 in. at top. Left side pillars should extend 5 in.; this will create the slightly tipped plate appearance. Position 6 in. plate.

Attach shoes to bodies with damp brush and position clowns. Add fondant to arms as needed to lengthen. Position hands. Shape bodies as needed. Remove heads and hands; let bodies stand to dry completely.

3. Draw mouths and eyebrows with black FoodWriter. Roll small balls, flatten and attach for eyes, pupils, cheeks. Roll and attach ball noses. Roll and flatten balls for ears and tongues; trim to shape and carve details with knife. Attach with damp brush. Make hair and hat trim: Yellow Clown: cut 2 blue strips 1/2 in. wide; cut 1/8 in. wide fringe on one edge and attach with damp brush, wrapping around head. Roll a 1/2 in. blue ball and insert on hat. Green Clown: cut 4 orange strips 1/2 in. wide and repeat fringe process; attach to head in layers with damp brush. Orange Clown: cut individual 1/8 in. wide yellow strips for hair; wrap around toothpick to curl and attach to head with damp brush. Make

hat pompom for Orange Clown. Cut a 1/4 in. wide blue strip; pinch ends to form a ruffle and attach to top of hat with damp brush.

Attach hats to heads with damp brush. Make ruffles (p. 109) for necks and legs; attach to body with damp brush. Roll and attach ball buttons and cuff trim. For Orange Clown shirt pompoms, cut 1/2 in. strips and cut fringe as for hair; roll ends together and attach with damp brush. Green Clown: cut a 1/4 in. wide yellow strip for collar; attach. Tie: roll yellow fondant 1/8 in. thick; cut a strip 3/4 in. wide, narrowing to 3/8 in. wide; cut 1/8 in. wide orange stripes and attach with damp brush. Roll small yellow ball for knot; attach knot and tie with damp brush. Attach hands when cake is assembled at reception.

Dream Doll House

A sweet fondant scene any little girl will love. The luscious landscaping could only be done with fondant—from the marbled walkway to the blossom umbrella to the shimmering flowers popping up everywhere.

Several days in advance: Make 2 fondant dolls* (see below); combining $1/2$ oz. neon pink with 10 oz. white fondant for pink dress. Reserve remaining pink. Make table, chairs, umbrella and stand, cups, saucers and flowers*. For table, cut white fondant circle using large round Cut-Out. Insert lollipop stick and pull out to form center hole. Let dry on cornstarch-dusted surface. For chair backs and seats, cut 4 white fondant circles using medium Cut-Out. Trim $1/2$ in. from chair back circles and attach to seats with thinned fondant; let dry. When dry, attach seats and backs to lollipop sticks, trimmed to $2^3/4$ in., using thinned fondant (p. 101). For cups and saucers, combine 2 oz. neon yellow with 4 oz. white fondant. Cut 2 saucers using smallest round Cut-Out. Roll two $1/4$ in. balls for cups; indent with small ball tool to form cup shape. Roll a thin $1/2$ in. long log for handle; curve and let dry. Attach handle to cup with thinned fondant.

For umbrella base, roll a $3/4$ in. white ball, flatten bottom; dampen a lollipop stick starting $2^1/2$ in. above bottom end and insert into umbrella base, leaving 2 in. extending below base; let dry. Cut neon pink combination umbrella with plastic flower cutter and let dry on back side of Mini Ball Pan dusted with cornstarch. Cut neon yellow center using medium round Cut-Out; attach to umbrella with damp brush and let dry. Make flowers using yellow, purple, orange and neon pink combination fondant (combine 1 oz. purple with 3 oz. white for purple, combine 1 oz. orange with 3 oz. white for orange). Roll out fondant $1/8$ in. thick and cut 5 flowers of each color using medium Cut-Out and 20 of each color using small Cut-Out. Brush flowers with water and sprinkle with Shimmer Dust (leave purple flowers plain); shake off excess. Roll small white ball flower centers and attach with damp brush. Let dry. Cut 20 lollipop sticks 3 in. high; spray with Color Mist. Attach sticks to medium flowers with thinned fondant. For leaves, knead green icing color into 2 oz. pastel green fondant. Cut leaves using small Cut-Out; brush with water and sprinkle with Shimmer Dust as above and let dry on small flower former. Attach leaves to sticks with thinned fondant. Attach table and umbrella to umbrella base with thinned fondant; let dry.

Prepare triple recipe of crisped rice cereal treats and spread 2 in. deep in sheet pan for base. Cover with green fondant; lightly smooth with Easy-Glide Smoother. Insert dowel rods, cut to height of cereal treats, where house will be positioned. Prepare house cake for rolled fondant by lightly icing with buttercream. Cover house with white fondant. Roll out fondant for purple door and yellow windows. Trace patterns with toothpick and cut out with craft knife; attach with damp brush. Using window patterns, cut pink curtains, imprint folds with veining tool and attach with damp brush. Cut purple shutters using medium heart Cut-Out; trim off bottom half and attach. Cut pink door window using small heart Cut-Out; attach. Roll yellow ball and teardrop door handle; attach. For door trim, roll $1/8$ in. neon pink combination balls, attach. For windowbox grass, roll $1/2$ in. ball of pastel green/kelly green combination fondant into a 2 in. log. Flatten one edge with rolling pin to extend $1/2$ in. and cut slits for grass with small scissors. Attach with damp brush, pulling out some grass to form leaves. Roll thin green logs for vines; attach at eaves. Attach small flowers on vines and windowboxes with damp brush. Cut pink roof shingles using medium heart Cut-Out; trim off point and attach in overlapping fashion with damp brush. For roof peak, cut 4 medium pink hearts. Brush backs of hearts with water and attach together in twos. Trim off $1/4$ in. at point of heart to level and attach upright with damp brush. Shape a $1^1/2$ in. rectangle chimney; attach a $1/2$ in. wide purple strip at top. Trim bottom at an angle to conform to roof, then attach to roof with damp brush. Attach additional flowers and handshaped leaves on roof.

For walkway, cut a 2 x 6 in. strip of white fondant, $1/4$ in. thick. Roll pink, yellow and white balls for stones, position over walkway and flatten with rolling pin. Attach with damp brush. For bushes, roll 1 in. green balls, flatten slightly and poke with veining tool to create a fluffed look. Attach around house and walkway. Attach flowers on stems to base sides with thinned fondant. For border grass, roll 1 in. green balls into 3 in. logs; repeat flattening and cutting process as for windowbox grass. Attach around base with thinned fondant. Position table, cups and saucers. Insert chair legs in cereal treat; position dolls.

Cake serves 12; cereal treats serve 12.

*****Note:** You will need to add Gum-Tex to fondant used for making dolls, table, chairs, umbrella, flowers and leaves. Use approximately $1/4$ to $1/2$ teaspoon per 4 oz. of fondant.

FONDANT DOLLS

1. Using neon yellow or pink combination fondant, form a $1^1/4$ in. high teardrop for body; flatten at top and bottom. Roll $3/8$ in. balls for sleeves; indent with ball tool to form cup shape. Using natural pink, roll a $7/8$ in. ball for head and a $1/8$ in. ball for neck. Make $1/4$ x $1^1/8$ in. log arms; indent end with craft knife to form fingers. Make $1/4$ x $1^1/4$ in. log legs; bend to form knee and ankle.

2. Construct dolls on waxed paper-covered craft block. Flatten neck and attach with damp brush. Carve a smile line in head with veining tool; attach head with damp brush. Attach legs with damp brush. Roll and cut a $5/8$ x 3 in. long skirt, gather slightly with fingers and attach to body with damp brush. Attach arms inside sleeves with damp brush, then attach to body.

3. Cut yellow or light brown strips for hair, $1/16$ x $1^1/4$ in. long. Wrap each strip around a toothpick to curl, then attach to head with damp brush. Roll small white and black balls for eyes and pupils and a small natural pink ball for nose; attach with damp brush. Attach small white strips around foot for shoes and straps. Let dry on craft block in seated position.

Final Dismissal

There's an easy way to help fondant decorations—like the graduates here—stand on their own two feet. Add our Gum-Tex to fondant before using to create an extra-firm texture. Use it on the locker doors and letters, too!

Project Checklist

- **Pans:** 8, 12 x 2 in. Square

- **Tip:** 2

- **Icing Colors:*** Lemon Yellow, Golden Yellow, Brown, Black

- **Fondant:** White Ready-To-Use Rolled Fondant (192 oz. needed), Fondant Multi Packs in Primary and Natural Colors (1 pk. each needed), People Cut-Outs™, Cutter/Embosser, Brush Set, Fine Tip Primary FoodWriters™, Perfect Height™ Rolling Pin, Roll & Cut Mat, Easy-Glide Fondant Smoother, p. 114-119

- **Recipe:** Buttercream Icing, Extra-Firm Rolled Fondant, p. 101

- **Also:** Gum-Tex™, p. 119; Piping Gel, 8 in. Lollipop Sticks, Cake Boards, Fanci-Foil Wrap, Wooden Dowel Rods, 101 Cookie Cutters Set, large heavy board (15 in. square x 1/2 in. thick), thin cardboard, small sharp knife, cornstarch

In advance: Cover prepared 15 in. square board with approximately 36 oz. of white rolled fondant (p. 99); smooth with Easy-Glide Smoother and set aside. To make graduates, books and message, add 1/2 teaspoon of Gum-Tex to each primary color fondant from Multi Pack. To make 14 graduates, create pattern by placing shirt and pants Cut-Outs on thin cardboard; trace around Cut-Outs and adjust pattern to form a 1-piece gown, then cut out pattern. Roll out blue fondant 1/8 in. thick, use pattern and sharp knife to cut gowns. Move arm portion up or down to create different arm positions. For shoes, roll out black fondant 1/8 in. thick and cut 14 pairs using Cut-Outs; immediately attach to gowns with damp brush. For 14 heads and pairs of hands, roll out light brown, dark brown and pink fondant 1/8 in. thick; cut with Cut-Outs. For hands, use shoe cutter, then cut piece in half (rounded end will be hand). Immediately attach hands and heads to gowns with damp brush. Let dry completely on cornstarch-dusted surface. When dry, pipe thinned fondant (p. 101) on back side at seams to reinforce. For 14 mortarboards, roll out blue fondant 1/8 in. thick and cut into 1 x 3/4 in. diamond shapes; let dry on cornstarch-dusted surface.

To make 12 books, roll out white fondant 1/4 in. thick and cut 1 x 1/2 in. rectangles. For covers, roll out red, yellow and green fondant 1/16 in. thick and cut rectangles a little larger to cover books; wrap around and trim to fit. Score lines for binding using Cutter/Embosser; let dry on cornstarch-dusted surface. For message, roll out red, green and blue fondant 1/8 in. thick and cut using alphabet cutters from set; also cut a comma shape using shoe Cut-Out, shape with fingers and immediately attach to "R" with damp brush. Let dry on cornstarch-dusted surface.

To tint fondant for lockers, knead a small amount of black fondant into 36 oz. of white fondant to create a medium gray shade. For inside of open lockers, add black fondant to 8 oz. of white fondant to create dark gray shade. To make open locker doors, add 1/2 teaspoon of Gum-Tex to 8 oz. of light gray fondant. Roll fondant 1/8 in. thick and cut 18 lockers, 1 1/4 in. x 4 in. high; let dry on cornstarch-dusted surface. Set aside remaining medium and dark gray fondant.

When graduates are dry, shape a small fondant cone brace, 3/4 in. high, for each leg and attach to back of shoes with damp brush. Let dry on cornstarch-dusted surface. When message letters are dry, attach lollipop sticks to back with thinned fondant; let dry.

Prepare 2-layer square cakes for stacked construction (p. 99) and place on same-sized boards. Prepare cakes for rolled fondant by lightly icing with buttercream. Cover cakes with white fondant (108 oz. needed to cover both cakes); smooth with Easy-Glide Smoother. Position cakes on prepared fondant-covered board. Make sets of 2 or 3 closed lockers using medium gray fondant, multiplying by the width of a single open locker. Attach closed lockers to cake sides with damp brush. Score closed locker sections with Cutter/Embosser for look of separate lockers, 1 1/4 in. wide. Cut dark gray inner open locker sections, same size as single lockers and attach between closed lockers with damp brush. For all locker doors, pipe tip 2 string† handles and vent lines in buttercream. Attach open locker doors at a slight angle, between closed locker sections, with thinned light gray fondant.

Draw facial features on graduates with black FoodWriter. In buttercream, pipe tip 2 string hair and pipe-in collar; attach mortarboards. Pipe tip 2 string tassel with pull-out fringe and dot button. Position graduates and books on cake. Insert message on cake top, cutting sticks as needed. For streamers, cut 4 or 6 in. long x 1/8 in. wide strips of fondant in assorted colors. Wrap around lollipop stick and slide onto cake. **Serves 68.**

***Note:** Combine Lemon Yellow and Golden Yellow for shade shown.

†Note: For instructions on specific piping techniques, see the Wilton Yearbook of Cake Decorating or visit www.wilton.com.

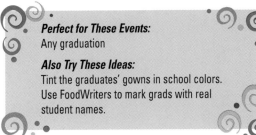

Perfect for These Events:
Any graduation

Also Try These Ideas:
Tint the graduates' gowns in school colors. Use FoodWriters to mark grads with real student names.

Aqua Impressions

Our fondant punches create a highly detailed design in one easy motion. You can see it on the accent strips here — pretty openwork diamonds are surrounded by fine-line scallops, which look great against the textured fondant overlay.

Project Checklist

- **Pan:** 10 x 2 in. Square

- **Fondant:** Ready-To-Use Rolled Fondant in Pastel Blue (96 oz. needed) and White (24 oz. needed), Fondant Decorative Punch Set, Cutter/Embosser, Brush Set, Perfect Height™ Rolling Pin, Roll & Cut Mat, Easy-Glide Fondant Smoother, p. 114-119

- **Recipe:** Buttercream Icing, p. 101

- **Also:** Overlay Flap Pattern, p. 113; pizza cutter, ruler, toothpick

Prepare 2-layer cake for rolled fondant by lightly icing with buttercream. Roll out blue fondant $1/8$ in. thick and cover cake (p. 98); smooth with Easy-Glide Smoother. For each side of cake, cut a 4 x 20 in. long strip of fondant to place under overlay flaps. Using straight-edge wheel of Cutter/Embosser, lightly imprint horizontal lines across strip, $1/4$ in. apart. Trim strips to 19 in. long. Turn over strips, smooth side up, fold ends back to meet in center; attach ends with damp brush. Attach strips, seam sides down, to cake sides, centering between corners.

Roll out blue fondant $1/4$ in. thick. Cut a 19 in. square for overlay. With toothpick, mark a 10 in. square in center. Using pattern, cut flaps on all four sides of square. Mark an 8 in. square at center of the trimmed overlay. Using Cutter/Embosser, score vertical lines, $1/2$ in. apart, leaving 8 in. center square plain. Position overlay on cake. Knead white fondant into remaining blue fondant to lighten. Roll out $1/8$ in. thick and cut 4 strips, 1 x 9 in. long. Using narrow diamond punch, punch out 5 designs, starting from center of strip to ends. Position strips on cake top and trim to 8 in. long, cutting corners at an angle to fit with other strips. Attach with damp brush. Repeat process, cutting 2 strips for each side of cake. Using a damp brush, attach diagonally from center of each side. Cut 1 x $1/4$ in. wide strips for each meeting point of strips; attach with damp brush. For monogram, cut $1/4$ in. wide strips of fondant and position in letter form on cake top.
Serves 30.

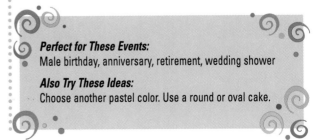

Perfect for These Events:
Male birthday, anniversary, retirement, wedding shower

Also Try These Ideas:
Choose another pastel color. Use a round or oval cake.

Wishing You Well

The charming stone well takes you back to simpler times. The marbleized stones, the overlapping fondant shingle roof and the sweetly shaped bluebird create a look that works for so many occasions.

Project Checklist

- **Pan:** 8 x 2 in. Round

- **Icing Colors:** Moss Green, Brown, Red-Red, Royal Blue, Golden Yellow

- **Fondant:** White Ready-To-Use Rolled Fondant (72 oz. needed), Neon Fondant Multi-Pack, Round Cut-Outs™, Fondant Shaping Foam, Fine Tip Primary FoodWriters™, Brush Set, Wide Glide™ Rolling Pin, Roll & Cut Mat, Easy-Glide Fondant Smoother, p. 114-119

- **Recipe:** Buttercream Icing, p. 101

- **Also:** Floral Collection Flower Making Set, Flower Former Set, Gum-Tex™, p. 114-119; Piping Gel, 10 in. Round Silver Cake Base, 6 in. Cookie Treat Sticks, Plastic Dowel Rods, 10 x 14 in. Cake Board, sharp knife, 1/4 in. wide white satin ribbon (8 in. needed), scissors, ruler, cornstarch

In advance: Make fondant bird (see below). Make shingles, bucket, flowers and leaves. For shingles, tint 24 oz. of fondant light brown, combined with a small amount of red-red. Knead in 1 teaspoon of Gum-Tex. Roll out 1/16 in. thick and cut 64 shingles, 1 x 2 in. wide. Let dry overnight on cornstarch-dusted surface. For bucket, roll brown/red-red fondant 1/4 in. thick and cut bottom using medium round Cut-Out. Roll fondant 1/8 in. thick and cut a 1 1/4 in. wide strip, long enough to wrap around base of circle; attach to circle with damp brush. Roll a 1/4 x 3 3/4 in. log and shape into handle; attach with damp brush and let dry.

For flowers, make yellow by combining a 1/2 in. ball of neon yellow with 4 oz. white fondant, make dark pink and light pink by combining 3 oz. each of neon pink with small amounts of white. For leaves, tint 2 oz. white with moss green icing color. Knead 1/4 teaspoon of Gum-Tex into each color. Using cutters from floral collection set, cut 79 pansies (45 dark pink, 24 light pink, 10 yellow),

46 apple blossoms (16 dark pink, 20 light pink, 10 yellow) and 47 forget-me-nots (14 dark pink, 33 light pink). Cup flowers and thin petals using ball tool from set. Let dry on flower formers dusted with cornstarch. Cut 60 moss green leaves using small rose leaf cutter from set and shaping foam. Thin edges of leaves with ball tool and trace veins with veining tool. Let dry on flower formers dusted with cornstarch.

For roof, cut cake board to 8 x 9 in. Score middle with knife to make 4 1/2 x 8 in. halves; bend board in half and brush outside with piping gel. Roll out brown/red-red fondant 1/8 in. thick and cover roof. For roof frame, cut a hole the diameter of a cookie stick on side of two plastic dowel rods, 5 in. from top. Cut cookie stick to 5 1/2 in. long and insert into holes so that rods are positioned 4 1/2 in. apart.

Prepare 2-layer cake for rolled fondant by lightly icing with buttercream. Cover cake and smooth with Easy-Glide Smoother. Attach shingles to roof with damp brush, overlapping so

that 1/2 in. of shingle is exposed in each row. Cut shingles to fit with scissors. Insert roof frame into cake top. Insert a 1/2 in. ball of brown/red-red fondant into top of each dowel rod. Position roof on frame.

For each marbleized stone, gently blend a 1/8 in. ball of brown/red-red fondant with a 1/2 in. ball of white fondant. Flatten stones to create irregular shapes. Attach stones to sides and extending 1/2 in. on top edge of cake with damp brush. Attach flowers and leaves to cake base, bucket and roof with icing. Attach bird with icing. Position bucket on top center of cake and tie to roof frame with ribbon.

Serves 20.

Perfect for These Events:
Wedding shower, female birthday, outdoor party centerpiece

Also Try These Ideas:
Make it a landscape cake by stacking with a sheet cake decorated with grass. Change flower styles and colors.

FONDANT BIRD

1. Tint a 2 1/2 in. ball of fondant blue. Shape a 1 1/2 in. high teardrop for body.

2. Flatten teardrop point and cut notches for tail feathers with craft knife. Roll a 3/4 in. ball for head; attach with damp brush. Shape 2 small teardrops and flatten for wings; cut notches for feathers and attach with damp brush.

3. Cut a small white circle for breast, score feather lines with knife and attach. For beak, tint a small ball golden yellow. Shape a small cone and attach with damp brush. Draw dots for eyes with black FoodWriter.

Over the Moon with Joy

These bouncing babies are cute as a button—and the buttons are pretty cute too! It's easy to give each baby its own personality, through details like pacifiers, bows, jumper colors and facial features. The quilted cake behind the babies is an easy effect created with the Cutter/Embosser.

Project Checklist

- **Pans:** 6, 10 x 2 in. Round
- **Fondant:** Ready-To-Use Rolled Fondant in White (96 oz. needed) and Pastel Yellow (24 oz. needed), Fondant Multi Packs in Natural and Pastel Colors (1 pk. each needed), Round and Star Cut-Outs™, Cutter/Embosser, Brush Set, Perfect Height™ Rolling Pin, Roll & Cut Mat, Easy-Glide Fondant Smoother, p. 114-119
- **Recipe:** Buttercream Icing, p. 101
- **Also:** Confectionery Tool Set, Gum-Tex™, p. 118-119; 101 Cookie Cutters Set, 11³/4 in. Lollipop Sticks, 14 in. Cake Circles (3 needed), Fanci-Foil Wrap, Piping Gel, confectioner's sugar, craft knife, ruler, wooden skewer, 4¹/2 in. circle or bowl, pencil with eraser, cornstarch, 12 x 4 x 4 in. high craft block, waxed paper

In advance: Prepare base board. Tape together three 14 in. cake circles. Cover prepared board with 24 oz. of white fondant (p. 99) and smooth with Easy-Glide Smoother. Make fondant babies following instructions below. Make moon and stars. For stars, knead ¹/2 teaspoon Gum-Tex into a 3 in. ball of pastel yellow fondant. Roll out ¹/8 in. thick and cut 2 stars using medium star Cut-Out; let dry on cornstarch-dusted surface. For moon, roll out remaining mixture and cut a curve using 5 in. bowl or circle as pattern. Move pattern out from curve and cut crescent shape, 1³/4 in. wide at widest point, to form moon; let dry on cornstarch-dusted surface. Cut 11 in., 10 in. and 6 in. lengths of lollipop sticks. Using thinned fondant (p. 101), attach moon to 6 in. stick and stars to other sticks. Let dry.

Prepare 2-layer 6 in. and 10 in. cakes for stacked construction (p. 99). Prepare cakes for rolled fondant by lightly icing with buttercream. Combine 36 oz. white with 18 oz. pastel yellow fondant. Cover cakes with fondant (p. 97); smooth with Easy-Glide Smoother. On 10 in. cake, use straight-edge wheel of Cutter/Embosser to imprint 3 in. x 2¹/2 in. diamond pattern around cake sides. Roll out white fondant ¹/8 in. thick and cut 24 circles for buttons using smallest round Cut-Out. Indent centers with dog bone tool from confectionery set; insert wooden skewer to form 2 buttonholes. Attach buttons at diamond points with damp brush. For "BABY" message on 6 in. cake, roll out pastel fondant ¹/8 in. thick and cut letters using cookie cutters; attach to cake with damp brush. Roll ³/8 in. white fondant balls and attach to bottom border of 6 in. cake with damp brush. Position babies on cake top and sides. For sleeping baby, roll out white fondant ¹/8 in. thick and cut a 3 in. square blanket. Imprint edges with Cutter/ Embosser and position over baby. Roll ³/8 in. white balls and attach between babies on 10 in. cake with damp brush. Insert stars and moon into cake.

Serves 40.

Perfect for These Events:
Baby shower, christening, pre-school graduation, playgroup party

Also Try These Ideas:
Add fondant baseball caps for boys, sunbonnets for girls. Replace buttons with fondant flowers.

3-D BABIES

1. Cover craft block with waxed paper and pin block to a waxed paper-covered board. Build babies against block, making all body parts before assembling. Roll 5 ball heads, 1 in. diameter, in natural pink fondant; flatten backs for babies with green, yellow and blue outfits. For outfits/bodies, roll 1¹/8 in. diameter balls in each color, form a 1¹/4 in. long pear shape; for sleeping baby, form a 2 in. long pear shape. Indent sides with ball tool and mark stitching dots with craft knife. For green outfit baby, roll ⁵/8 in. ball short sleeves. For all arms and legs, roll ³/8 x 1 in. long logs; for legs, indent center for knee and back for heel, curve up end to form foot. Carve toes with knife. For all but green baby, roll ³/8 in. balls for hands; flatten and carve out notch for thumb and indent lines for fingers. For green outfit baby, flatten end of arm for hand and repeat procedure for fingers and thumbs.

2. Assemble using a damp brush. Position body then attach legs, sleeves/arms, hands and head to create various poses. Roll tiny ball for nose; attach with damp brush. Indent eye sockets with end of veining tool. Carve mouth with veining tool; smooth.

3. Roll small logs for collars. Use veining tool to create ruffles or notches; attach. For bow, roll a small pink ball; indent and shape into bow. Attach to head of crawling baby. Roll and attach small white and black balls for eyes and pupils.

Indent lashes with craft knife. For ears, roll and flatten a tiny pink ball, cut in half, indent with veining tool and attach. For pacifier, roll and flatten a tiny white ball, roll another white ball and attach on top; attach to head. For hair, cut thin strips of brown fondant and attach. When cake is complete, attach babies with damp brush.

89

Botanical Beauty

Use the right tool for the job and your work is easy. Our Square Cut-Outs™ are the right tool for making this fondant lattice fence. Simply cut out the squares following the spacing pattern—you'll finish with a precisely cut panel with the seamless look you want.

Project Checklist

- **Pans:** Hexagon Set (9, 15 x 2 in. used)

- **Fondant:** Ready-To-Use Rolled Fondant in White (120 oz. needed) and Pastel Green (96 oz. needed), Pastel Colors Fondant Multi Pack, Square Cut-Outs™, Fondant Shaping Foam, Wide Glide™ Rolling Pin, Roll & Cut Mat, Easy-Glide Fondant Smoother, p. 114-119

- **Recipe:** Buttercream Icing, p. 101

- **Also:** Lattice Spacing Pattern, Angle Guide Pattern, p. 113; Gum-Tex™, Floral Collection Flower Making Set, Confectionery Tool Set, Flower Former Set, p. 118-119; Cake Boards, Fanci-Foil Wrap, Hidden Pillars, Wooden Dowel Rods, Piping Gel, Pastry Brush, 22-gauge cloth-coated florist wire, 3 in. foil squares, cornstarch, craft block

In advance: Make fondant flowers and leaves. Add $1/2$ teaspoon Gum-Tex to each 4 oz. of fondant. Cut 70 leaves using small rose leaf cutter from flower making set; imprint veins with veining tool. Attach 20 leaves to wires by lightly brushing backs with thinned fondant (p. 101) and pressing wires into backs of vein lines. Pinch bottoms of leaves to seal around wire. Insert wired leaves into craft block to dry; let remaining leaves dry on cornstarch-dusted flower formers. Combine $1^1/2$ oz. each of pastel pink and pastel yellow fondant to create peach color. Cut approximately 120 flowers in assorted pastel colors and white using small and large daisy, apple blossom and pansy cutters from set. Using ball tool and shaping foam, thin edges of flowers slightly and cup centers. Let dry on crumpled foil squares dusted with cornstarch to create a natural look. Prepare 50 wires for flowers. Bend a $1/8$ in. hook at 90° angle at one end. For flower centers, roll a small ball of fondant (white for pastel, yellow for white flowers), flatten slightly. Dip wire hook in water and insert ball center on hook, pinch bottom to seal ball center to wire and let dry. When dry, attach 50 flowers to wires. Push straight end of wire through middle of flowers and slide flower up toward ball center. Attach with thinned fondant. Set aside to dry.

Also in advance: Prepare base board. Combine 48 oz. of pastel green with 24 oz. of white fondant; reserve half of mixture. Cut 3 cake boards 1 in. larger than 15 in. hexagon pan, tape together. Cover prepared board with fondant (p. 99) and smooth with Easy-Glide Smoother.

To cover cakes, combine 48 oz. of pastel green with 24 oz. white fondant; knead in reserved fondant mixture. Prepare 2-layer 9 and 15 in. hexagon cakes (bake two $1^1/2$ in. high layers to make each 3 in. high cake) for stacked construction (p. 99). Prepare cakes for rolled fondant by lightly icing with buttercream. Cover cakes with fondant; smooth with Easy-Glide Smoother. Cover top 3 in. of hidden pillar with fondant to create bouquet vase; set aside. Position cakes on prepared base board.

Make lattice panels using spacing pattern (see instructions below). Attach panels to sides with damp brush, lining up fondant where panels meet. For hidden pillar vase, repeat lattice process, using a 3 in. strip of fondant. Attach to fondant-covered portion of pillar with damp brush.

Insert pillar until fondant-covered portion meets cake top. Roll a small log of fondant and wrap around base of pillar. Place a ball of fondant inside pillar to secure bouquet flowers. Insert flowers and leaves on wires in pillar. Attach remaining flowers and leaves to cake corners with buttercream. **Serves 68.**

Perfect for These Events:
Mother's Day, wedding or anniversary, garden party

Also Try These Ideas:
For showers, make extra fondant flowers to accent favors and napkin rings. Use round or square cakes, if desired.

LATTICE PANELS

1. Roll fondant $1/8$ in. thick on surface lightly dusted with cornstarch. To ensure that panels line up at bottom, make 3 panels at a time; cut a piece $3^1/2$ in. high x 14 in. wide for 9 in. cake, cut a piece $3^1/2$ in. high x $15^1/2$ in. wide for 15 in.

cake. Position pattern at top left corner at a 45° angle using Angle Guide Pattern. Using smallest square Cut-Out, cut squares between lines on pattern at its bottom edge. Remove cut squares.

2. Move pattern below cut area and repeat process. Continue until entire panel is cut out.

3. Cut strip to desired width of each hexagon side. Repeat process to create a panel for each side.

Captivating Cameos

It's a more formal cake that really lets loose with texture! The cameos are edged with forget-me-nots and imprinted with a pretty floral design. Add multi-layered blossoms flowering from each tier and a burst of wired flowers on top, and this design definitely has the "wow" factor.

Project Checklist

- **Pans:** 8,10,12 x 2 in. Round
- **Icing Color:** Ivory
- **Fondant:** White Ready-To-Use Rolled Fondant (312 oz. needed), Oval Cut-Outs™; 9-Pc. Fondant Punch Set, Brush Set, Fondant Shaping Foam, Perfect Height™ Rolling Pin, Wide Glide™ Rolling Pin, Roll & Cut Mat, Easy-Glide Fondant Smoother, p. 114-119
- **Recipe:** Buttercream Icing, p. 101
- **Also:** Confectionery Tool Set, Stepsaving Rose Bouquets Flower Cutter Set* (small and large rose cutters needed), Floral Collection Flower Making Set (forget-me-not cutter needed), Candy Melting Plate (5 needed), Gum-Tex™, p. 118-119; Cake Dividing Set, Cake Circles, Fanci-Foil Wrap, 16 in. Silver Cake Base, Hidden Pillars, Wooden Dowel Rods, 24-gauge white cloth-coated florist wires (11 in. lengths, 30 needed), cornstarch, paring knife, craft block

  *Or use large and medium Flower Cut-Outs™, p. 115

At least 2 weeks in advance: Make fondant flowers. Knead 2 teaspoons Gum-Tex into 24 oz. white fondant and follow instructions at bottom of page. For rose petal flowers, you will need 89 large 2-layer flowers, 10 large 1-layer flowers, 49 small 2-layer flowers and 120 small 1-layer flowers. For forget-me-nots, you will need approximately 360 to be placed around oval cameos; 160 additional forget-me-nots will be placed on wires. Immediately after cutting and shaping, brush bottom edge with water; fold flowers in half and wrap around wire. Pinch bottom to secure. Position flowers 1 1/2 in. apart, 5 or 6 per wire. Let dry in craft block.

In advance: Prepare base board. Tint 252 oz. fondant ivory. Lightly brush silver cake base with piping gel. Cover with 24 oz. of fondant (p. 99) and smooth with Easy-Glide Smoother. Reserve remaining ivory fondant for covering all cakes.

Prepare 3-layer cakes (make three 2 in. layers of each size cake to make 6 in. high cakes) for stacked construction (see p. 99). Prepare cakes for rolled fondant by lightly icing with buttercream. Cover cakes with fondant; smooth with Easy-Glide Smoother. Reserve remaining ivory fondant (approximately 16 oz.). Using Cake Dividing Set, divide 8 in. cake into 6ths, 10 in. cake into 8ths, 12 in. cake into 10ths. Assemble cakes on fondant-covered base. Cut 1/2 in. wide x 7 in. long strips of white fondant. Attach to cake sides at division marks with damp brush. Roll 1/4 in. balls of white fondant and attach 3/4 in. apart on strips with damp brush.

For swags around bottom tier, cut ten 5 in. square pieces of white fondant. Pleat and drape swags; attach to cake at division points with damp brush; then attach a large 1-layer flower. For 24 ovals, roll out white fondant 1/16 in. thick and cut with large oval Cut-Out; cut out and imprint center design using Snapdragon punch. Roll out reserved ivory fondant 1/16 in. thick and cut with large oval Cut-Out; attach ivory oval to back of white oval with damp brush. Attach ovals to cake sides between white fondant strips. Attach unwired forget-me-nots around ovals with thinned fondant; you may need to trim off pinched backs to allow flowers to lay flat. Insert hidden pillar completely in top tier and place a small ball of fondant inside to secure flowers. With thinned fondant, attach rose petal flowers covering cake top and top edges of other cakes; trim off pinched backs if needed. Insert wired flowers in hidden pillar.

Serves 94.*

***Note:** For wedding cakes, the smallest tier is often saved for the first anniversary. The number of servings given does not include the smallest tier.

Perfect for These Events:
Wedding, anniversary

Also Try These Ideas:
Use a white-on-white or pastel color treatment. Add pastel chalk to flowers for a subtle touch of color.

ROSE PETAL FLOWERS AND FORGET-ME-NOTS

The 2-layer rose petal flowers are shown in this sequence. For 1-layer rose petal flowers, just make the inner 1st layer. For forget-me-nots, follow steps for the inner 1st layer, but use the forget-me-not cutter and do not cut slits between petals.

1. Roll out fondant 1/16 in. thick. Using large or small rose cutter, cut out flower. Cut a small slit, 1/4 in. for small flowers, 1/2 in. for large, between each petal. On shaping foam, thin edges with ball tool from confectionery set. Brush center with water.

2. Pinch bottom center of flower so that petals naturally rise. Lightly push in sides of one petal, then another, so that you create a 2-petal center. For forget-me-nots to be placed on wires, immediately attach following cake instructions above. Let other flowers dry in candy melting plate cavity for 1 hour, then place on cornstarch-dusted cookie sheets to dry overnight.

3. For outer layer of rose petal flowers, cut a same size flower and thin edge with ball tool. Using dogbone tool from confectionery set, poke small hole in center; brush with water. Slide this flower over pinched bottom of inner layer flower. Let dry upside down to give outer layer a natural curl.

Put It in Writing <small>featured on page 8</small>

When a sheet cake looks this special, you can appreciate the power of fondant!
This design is a lucky combination of bright primary colors and fun cut-out shapes.

Project Checklist

- **Pans:** 11 x 15 x 2 in. Sheet
- **Fondant:** White Ready-To-Use Rolled Fondant (60 oz. needed), Primary Colors Fondant Multi Pack, Star and Round Cut-Outs™, Brush Set, Perfect Height™ Rolling Pin, Roll & Cut Mat, Easy-Glide Fondant Smoother, p. 114-119
- **Recipe:** Buttercream Icing, p. 101
- **Also:** 101 Cookie Cutters Set, Cake Boards, Fanci-Foil Wrap, paring knife

Prepare 1-layer cake for rolled fondant by lightly icing with buttercream. Cover with fondant and smooth with Easy-Glide Smoother. Combine 1 packet of blue fondant from Multi Pack with 2 oz. of white fondant. Roll out all colors 1/8 in. thick. Cut stars and circles in a variety of colors using small and medium Cut-Outs™; attach to cake with damp brush. For balloon strings, cut 1/8 in. wide fondant strips; attach with damp brush. Cut blue message with cookie cutters; attach to cake with damp brush. For bottom border, roll 1/2 in. balls of colored fondant and attach with damp brush.
Serves 30.

Perfect for These Events:
Any age birthday, graduation, retirement, promotion

Also Try These Ideas:
Personalize with a name using Cut-Outs. Transfer the design to round or square cakes. Use pastel colors for a shower.

Attract a Crowd <small>featured on page 32</small>

Smaller cakes add just the right note of color at each reception table. The butterflies are actually fondant hearts—make extras to land on everyone's plate.

Project Checklist

- **Pans:** Petal Pan Set (6 in. pan used)
- **Fondant:** Ready-To-Use Rolled Fondant in White, Pastel Yellow and Pastel Pink (24 oz. each needed), Neon and Primary Colors Fondant Multi Packs (1 pk. each needed), Brush-On Color™ in Pink, Yellow and Violet; Heart and Daisy Cut-Outs™, Brush Set, Perfect Height™ Rolling Pin, Roll & Cut Mat, p. 114-119
- **Recipe:** Buttercream Icing, p. 101
- **Also:** Gum-Tex™, p. 119; Confectionery Tool Set, p. 118; Cake Boards, craft knife, ruler, paper towels, cornstarch

3 or 4 days in advance: Make butterflies. Separately knead 1 in. balls of neon yellow and neon pink fondant with 1/2 teaspoon of Gum-Tex each. Knead a 1/2 in. ball of neon purple fondant with 1/4 teaspoon of Gum-Tex. For wings, roll out yellow and pink fondant 1/8 in. thick. Using large Cut-Out, cut 2 pink hearts for each butterfly; using medium Cut-Out, cut 2 yellow hearts for each butterfly. Attach yellow to pink heart with damp brush. With craft knife, trim 5/8 in. from bottom of hearts. For antennas, roll very thin 3/8 in. long logs of purple fondant; attach tiny balls at one end with damp brush. Reserve remaining purple fondant. Let all dry on cornstarch-dusted surface. When wings are dry, attach 2 sets together with thinned fondant (p. 101). Prop at an angle with crumpled paper towels and let dry.

To cover cakes, separately mix 6 oz. portions of white fondant with 6 oz. pastel yellow, 6 oz. pastel pink and a 1 in. ball of neon purple fondant. Also mix 1 1/2 in. balls of neon violet, neon yellow and neon pink fondant with 1 1/2 in. balls of white. For green color, mix a 1 1/2 in. ball of primary green with a 2 in. ball of white and a 1 in. ball of neon yellow.

Prepare 1-layer cakes for rolled fondant by lightly icing with buttercream. Cover cakes with the pastel purple, yellow and pink fondant mixtures; smooth. Using sponging technique (p. 105), dab cake tops with matching Brush-On Color. Mark center of cake tops with knife. Using matching neon colors, roll 1/4 x 4 in. long logs. Form loops and position at each petal division. Leave a 1/2 in. opening at each flower center. Roll out matching neon colors 1/8 in. thick and cut a large and medium daisy for each flower center, using Cut-Outs. Insert daisies in center opening. Roll a 3/8 in. white ball and attach for flower center. Cut a 1/4 in. hole on cake sides, 1 in. from bottom. Using green fondant, roll 1/4 x 6 in. long logs for each stem; insert in hole. Roll out green fondant 1/8 in. thick and cut a free-form leaf with craft knife; use veining tool from set to create veins. Position on stem.

Using reserved purple fondant, roll a 1 1/4 in. long log for each butterfly body, and a 3/8 in. ball for each head. Attach to wings with thinned fondant. Attach antennas with thinned fondant. Position butterflies.
Each serves 3.

Perfect for These Events:
Wedding shower, girl's birthday, Mother's Day, tea party

Also Try These Ideas:
Make fondant bees instead of butterflies. Create other flower colors.

Checkerboard Chic
featured on page 54

With its textured fondant panels, achieved with the Ribbon Cutter/Embosser, this pure white cake can provide as much excitement as any boldly colored design.

featured on page 54

Project Checklist

- **Pans:** 6, 8, 10 x 2 in. Round

- **Fondant:** White Ready-To-Use Rolled Fondant (144 oz. needed), Ribbon Cutter/Embosser Set, Flower Cut-Outs™, Fondant Shaping Foam, Brush Set, Wide Glide™ Rolling Pin, Roll & Cut Mat, Easy-Glide Fondant Smoother, p. 114-119

- **Recipe:** Buttercream Icing, p. 101

- **Also:** Confectionery Tool Set, p. 118; Gum-Tex™, p. 119; 12 in. Round Silver Cake Base, Dowel Rods, Piping Gel, 3 in. foil squares, plastic ruler, paring knife, confectioner's sugar

Several days in advance: Make flowers. Knead 1 teaspoon of Gum-Tex™ into 12 oz. of fondant. Roll out fondant 1/8 in. thick and cut 14 flowers using large Cut-Out™ and 35 flowers using medium Cut-Out. Cup centers on thick foam using ball tool from Confectionery Set. Let dry on cupped foil squares dusted with cornstarch. For large flowers, roll 3/8 in. ball flower centers; for medium flowers roll 1/4 in. ball centers. Attach centers to flowers with thinned fondant (p. 101). To prepare cake base, lightly brush with piping gel, and cover with fondant (p. 99). Smooth with Easy-Glide Smoother.

Prepare 3-layer cakes (for each, bake two 2 in. and one 1 in. high layers to make a 5 in. high cake) for rolled fondant by lightly icing with buttercream. Prepare cakes for stacked construction (p. 99) and position on base. Cover cakes with fondant (p. 97); smooth with Easy-Glide Smoother.

Make embossed squares using Ribbon Cutter/ Embosser. Roll out fondant 3/16 in. thick. Using straight-edge cutters and 2 striped embossing wheels, cut into strips. Cut strips into 13/4 in. squares; you will need approximately 25 squares for 10 in. cake, 20 for 8 in. cake and 16 for 6 in. cake. Attach squares to cake sides in checkerboard fashion, with damp brush. For bottom borders, roll 1/4 in. balls of fondant and attach with thinned fondant. Attach flowers with thinned fondant.
Serves 62 (wedding-size servings)* or 60 (party-size servings).

*Note: The top tier is often saved for the first anniversary. The number of servings given does not include top tier.

Perfect for These Events:
Wedding, anniversary, birthday (1 tier), shower

Also Try These Ideas:
Cover in chocolate fondant for groom's cake or man's birthday. Use contrasting colors for embossed squares.

Layered in Luxury
featured on page 74

Everything you love about fondant comes together on this unforgettable garden cake. Soft pastel colors, a richly textured crisscross backdrop, precisely cut geometric accents and a perfectly shaped rose bouquet set a new standard for elegance.

featured on page 74

Project Checklist

- **Pans:** 8, 12 x 2 in. Square

- **Tip:** 2

- **Icing Colors:** Rose, Moss Green

- **Fondant:** Ready-To-Use Rolled Fondant in White (96 oz. needed), Pastel Green (144 oz. needed) and Pastel Pink (24 oz. needed), Fondant Ribbon Cutter/Embosser Set, Cutter/ Embosser, Round Cut-Outs™. Fondant Shaping Foam, Brush Set, Wide Glide™ Rolling Pin, Roll & Cut Mat, Easy-Glide Fondant Smoother, p. 114-119

- **Recipe:** Buttercream Icing, p. 101

- **Also:** Stepsaving Rose Bouquets Flower Cutter Set, Gum-Tex™, Confectionery Tool Set, Flower Former Set, p. 114-119; Wooden Dowel Rods, Fanci-Foil Wrap, Piping Gel, 14 in. square triple-thick cardboard or 1/2 in. thick foam core board, 18- and 22-gauge florist wire, light green florist tape, toothpicks, cornstarch; 1/2 in. wide x 24 in. long pink satin ribbon, scissors, ruler

At least 3 days in advance: Make 12 Full Bloom Roses (p. 111) for bouquet with calyxes and leaves. Knead 1 teaspoon of Gum-Tex into 12 oz. of Pastel Pink fondant; knead in Rose Icing Color for shade shown. Prepare bases on 7 in. lengths of 18-gauge wire; let dry for 2 days. When dry, use large rose cutter from Stepsaving Set and pink fondant mixture to complete roses. For leaves and calyxes, knead 1/2 teaspoon of Gum-Tex into a 21/2 in. ball of Pastel Green fondant; knead in Moss Green Icing Color for shade shown. Using calyx cutter from set, cut 12 calyxes and attach with damp brush. Using rose leaf cutter from set, cut 15 leaves. Vein leaves on thin shaping foam using veiner tool from Confectionery Set. Attach to 7 in. lengths of 22-gauge wire with damp brush; let dry. Wrap each wire with florist tape. Make 48 fondant circles. Roll out white fondant 1/8 in. thick and cut with medium round Cut-Out™; let dry on cornstarch-dusted surface. Make fifty 2-layer pink fantasy flowers, a few at a time. Cut 2 blossoms for each fantasy flower using forget-me-not cutter from set. For the 50 bottom layer blossoms, place on thin shaping foam and cut a 1/8 in. slit between each petal. Thin edges and widen petals with medium ball tool from confectionery set; place on small flower former. For the 50 top layer blossoms, place on thick shaping foam and cup centers with small ball tool. Attach cupped blossom to flat blossom with damp brush; let dry. Pipe tip 2 dot centers in buttercream.† Set aside.

Prepare base board. Wrap triple-thick cardboard or foam core base with foil. Lightly brush with piping gel. Cover board with fondant (p. 99) and smooth with Easy-Glide Smoother. Set aside.

Prepare 3-layer cakes (for each, bake two 2 in. and one 1 in. high layers to make a 5 in. high cake) for rolled fondant by lightly icing with buttercream. Prepare cakes for stacked construction (p. 99). Cover cakes with Pastel Green fondant (p. 98); smooth with Easy-Glide Smoother. On both cakes, use straight-edge wheel of Cutter/Embosser to emboss crisscrossing lines, 1/2 in. apart at a 45° angle. Make white fondant overlays. Roll out fondant 1/8 in. thick. For 8 in. cake, cut a 12 in. square, position on cake top and trim as needed to extend 11/2 in. from top edge. For 12 in. cake, cut a 16 in. square, position and trim as above. Position cakes on fondant-covered board. Make approximately 48 fondant strips for cake sides. Roll out fondant 1/8 in. thick. Load Ribbon Cutter/Embosser with straight cutting wheels on each side of 1/4 in. spacer. Cut strips 1/2 in. wide x 31/2 in. long. With damp brush, attach 1 strip at each corner of cakes. On 8 in. cake, attach 4 additional strips, 11/8 in. apart, on each side. On 12 in. cake, attach 6 additional strips, 13/4 in. apart, on each side. With thinned fondant, attach 5 fondant circles to each side of 8 in. cake and 7 circles to each side of 12 in. cake. Attach a fantasy flower to center of each circle with thinned fondant (p. 101). Roll 1/4 in. balls of white fondant; attach between circles and

randomly on overlay with thinned fondant. For bottom borders, roll 1/4 in. balls of Pastel Green fondant and attach with damp brush.

Assemble rose bouquet. Tape 3 roses and 3 leaves together 3 in. below bottom of flowers. Curve stems at bottom. Repeat process with remaining flowers and leaves to form 4 sets. Cut dowel rod to 9 in. long. Cover top 4 in. with florist tape. Tape 4 sets together around wrapped dowel rod, 1 in. from top. Tie ribbon around taped area of bouquet; trim ends at an angle. At reception, insert bouquet in center of cake top.
Serves 68.

†Note: For instructions on specific piping techniques, see the Wilton Yearbook of Cake Decorating or visit www.wilton.com.

Perfect for These Events:
Wedding shower, anniversary, birthday, graduation, retirement

Also Try These Ideas:
Cover the bottom tier in a different color fondant. Replace roses with your favorite fondant flowers.

Preparing the Cake

Most designs in this book start with a cake covered in fondant—so let's begin with one of the most important fondant fundamentals—getting the cake ready for the fondant. In order to end up with a perfectly smooth fondant surface, you need to create a perfectly level cake. Any bumps or gaps in the cake will show up in your fondant. Here is the best way to ensure your cake will be in perfect shape for its fondant covering.

Level and Fill Cakes

Start by baking a cake using firm-textured batter, such as pound cake or fruitcake. Let cake cool at least one hour, then level off the crown, using the Wilton Cake Leveler or a serrated knife. If you've baked two or more layers, level each layer.

1. Leveling. Using a Cake Leveler: Place cake on a cake circle. Position ends of the cutting wire into notches at desired height. With legs standing on work surface, cut into crusted edge using an easy sawing motion, then gently glide through cake.

Using a Serrated Knife: Place cake on a cake circle and then onto the Trim 'N Turn Decorating Turntable. While slowly rotating the turntable, move knife back and forth in a sawing motion to remove the crown. Make sure to keep the knife level as you cut.

2. Filling. The filling, usually buttercream icing, helps hold cake layers together and adds flavor. Fill a decorating bag with buttercream without placing a tip on the coupler, or use tip 12. Make a dam by squeezing out a circle of icing 1/4 in. from the outside edge of the cake. This will help prevent filling from seeping out. Fill inside the circle with icing, using the Small Angled Spatula to spread (preserves or pudding may also be used).

3. Place next layer on top, making sure it is level.

Ice Cakes

Before covering with fondant, cakes must be lightly iced to seal in moisture and to help fondant stick to the cake. There are two easy ways to ice.

Using the Cake Icer Tip.

1. This is the fastest way to get a smooth surface. Trim a 16 in. Featherweight decorating bag to fit tip 789. Fill bag half full. Starting in center of cake top, hold bag at a 45° angle, lightly pressing the serrated edge of tip against cake. Squeeze a ribbon of icing in a continuous spiral motion to cover cake top, with last ribbon forcing icing over the edge of cake top.

2. To ice the sides, squeeze icing as you turn the cake slowly on the Trim 'N Turn turntable. Repeat the process until the entire cake side is covered.

3. Smooth the sides of the cake by leveling the icing with the edge of the Large Angled Spatula. For easier smoothing, it may help to dip the spatula into hot water, wipe dry and glide it across the entire surface.

Smooth the top using the end of the spatula. Sweep the edge of the spatula from the rim of the cake to its center. Then lift it off and remove excess icing. Rotate the cake slightly and repeat the procedure, starting from a new point on the rim until you have smoothed the entire top surface.

Using a Large Angled Spatula.

1. Gliding your spatula on the icing is the trick to keeping crumbs out of the icing. Never allow your spatula to touch the cake surface. Place a large amount of icing on the center of the cake top.

2. Cover sides with icing. Create smooth sides by holding the spatula upright with its edge against the side. Slowly spin the Trim 'N Turn turntable without lifting the

Spread across the top, pushing toward the edges.

spatula from the icing surface. Return excess icing to the bowl and repeat until sides are smooth.

3. Smooth the sides and top with the spatula, following step 3 for "Using the Cake Icer Tip" above.

Covering Round Cakes

How do you cover a cake with fondant that's perfectly smooth, without wrinkles or air bubbles? The flexibility of fondant is your secret weapon. Just follow our instructions for the right ways to knead, roll out and lift the fondant, and you'll find that covering a cake is easy.

1. Prepare cake by covering with buttercream icing.

2. Before rolling out fondant, knead it until it is a workable consistency. If fondant is sticky, knead in a little confectioner's sugar. Lightly

dust your smooth work surface or the Roll & Cut Mat and your rolling pin with confectioner's sugar to prevent sticking. Roll out fondant sized to your cake (see "Calculating the Size," p. 100).

To keep fondant from sticking, lift and move as you roll. Add more confectioner's sugar if needed.

3. Gently lift fondant over rolling pin and position on cake.

4. Shape fondant to sides of cake with Easy-Glide Smoother. We recommend using the Smoother because the pressure of your hands may leave impressions on the fondant.

Use the straight edge of the Smoother to mark fondant at the base of cake. Trim off excess

fondant using a spatula or sharp knife.

5. Smooth and shape fondant on cake using Easy-Glide Smoother. Beginning in the middle of the cake top, move the Smoother outward and down the sides to smooth and shape fondant to the cake and remove air

bubbles. If an air bubble appears, insert a pin on an angle, release air and smooth the area again.

6. Your cake is now ready to decorate.

Covering Large Round Cakes

Cakes 14 in. and larger require extra care in covering. Don't use a rolling pin to lift the larger amount of fondant needed. Instead, use the safer cake board method described here.

1. Cover cake with buttercream icing. Roll out fondant sized to your cake.

2. Slide a large cake circle that has been dusted with confectioner's sugar under the rolled fondant. Lift the circle and the fondant and position over

your cake. Gently shake the circle to slide the fondant off the board and into position on the cake.

3. Smooth and trim as described in "Covering Round Cakes" in instructions above.

> **SUCCESS TIP:**
>
> *Use the Roll & Cut Mat to roll out your fondant. It's the ideal smooth surface for rolling. Best of all, with the mat's pre-marked circles, it's easy to roll the exact size you need. Whenever you are handling fondant, be sure your hands are clean and dry.*

Covering Square Cakes

Don't let the sharp corners of a square cake intimidate you. It's easy to use your hands to shape fondant around the corners, so you finish with perfectly smooth edges.

1. Position fondant on cake, smoothing the top with the Easy-Glide Smoother. Pull the corner flaps gently out and away from the cake; smooth the corners with hand to eliminate the creases. Smooth sides with Smoother.

2. Trim off excess fondant at bottom with a spatula or sharp knife.

3. To give a finished look, smooth top, all sides and bottom edge of cake again with the Smoother.

Covering Petal & Star Cakes

After you've met the challenge of the petal's rounded divisions and the star's pointed ends, you'll be ready to successfully cover the heart, which combines both features.

1. Position fondant on cake, smoothing the top with the Easy-Glide Smoother. Form a cupped shape with your hand and gently smooth each petal division from top edge downward.

2. Trim off excess fondant at bottom with a spatula or a sharp knife.

3. Smooth out bottom edge.

1. Position fondant on cake, smoothing the top with the Easy-Glide Smoother. Form a right angle between your thumb and index finger and gently smooth fondant around each star point.

2. Trim off excess fondant at bottom with a spatula.

3. Smooth out sides and bottom edge with the Smoother.

Covering Base Boards

Give your cake a dramatic look by placing it on a base board covered with fondant. Cut cake boards 2 in. larger in diameter than your cake, unless otherwise directed, then roll out fondant about 1 in. larger than board size. Wrap board with foil.

1. Lightly coat board with piping gel to help the fondant stick to the foil.

2. Roll out fondant to desired size, 1/4 in. thick. Position over board using a rolling pin, draping fondant over edge.

3. Trim excess fondant from edges under bottom of board. Smooth top and sides with Easy-Glide Smoother.

Stacked Construction

In this most popular method of cake construction, cakes are placed directly on top of one another to create a great architectural look. The cakes must be supported and stabilized by dowel rods and cake boards, cut to size. After you've covered each cake with fondant, it's time to prepare them for stacked construction.

HOW MANY DOWEL RODS DO YOU NEED?

The larger the cake you're supporting, the more dowel rods you'll need. If the top cake is 10 in. or less, use 6 1/4 in. wooden dowel rods or 4 white plastic dowel rods. For 16 and 18 in. cakes, use 8 dowel rods—we recommend the wider plastic dowel rods for these larger cakes because they provide more support.

1. Mark the bottom cake for placement of dowel rods. This is done using the cake above it for size reference. Center a cake board the same size as the cake above it on the base cake. Using a toothpick, trace the board edge; dowel rods will be placed within this traced outline.

2. Insert one dowel rod into cake, straight down to the cake board. Make a knife scratch on the dowel rod to mark the exact height. Pull out dowel rod.

3. Cut the suggested number of dowel rods (see note at left) the exact same height, using the marked dowel rod as a guide.

4. Insert dowel rods into cake, spacing evenly 1 1/2 inches in from the imprinted outline. Push straight down until each rod touches the cake board. Repeat procedure for every stacked cake used, except top cake.

5. Position next smallest cake on bottom cake, centering exactly. Position any other cakes in the same way. To stabilize cakes further, sharpen one end of a longer dowel rod and push it through all cakes and boards to the base of the bottom cake.

6. Your stacked cake is ready for decorating, starting from the top tier down.

The Right Amount of Fondant for Your Cake

Use this chart to determine how much Wilton Ready-To-Use Rolled Fondant to buy for covering cakes. Additional fondant may be needed for decorations, depending on design. Wilton White Fondant is available in 24 oz. and 80 oz. packages; our pre-tinted fondant is available in 24 oz. packages.

CALCULATING THE SIZE:

Here's the easy formula for figuring the size you need to roll fondant to cover a round, square or sheet cake. Measure top of cake across center and add height of each side. Roll out fondant to that size, 1/4 in. thick.

For example, 8 in. 2-layer cake: 8 in. top + two 4 in. sides = 16 in. diameter fondant. For petals, ovals, hearts and hexagons, you would use the same formula—just remember to measure at the widest area of the top of the cake to determine the size.

Cake Shapes	Cake Size	Use This Amount
Rounds • 4 in. high	6 in.	18 oz.
	8 in.	24 oz.
	10 in.	36 oz.
	12 in.	48 oz.
	14 in.	72 oz.
	16 in.	108 oz.
Rounds • 3 in. high	6 in.	14 oz.
	8 in.	18 oz.
	10 in.	24 in.
	12 in.	36 oz.
	14 in.	48 oz.
	16 in.	72 oz.
Sheets • 2 in. high	7 x 11 in.	30 oz.
	9 x 13 in.	40 oz.
	11 x 15 in.	60 oz.
	12 x 18 in.	80 oz.
Ovals • 4 in. high	7 x 5 in.	24 oz.
	10 x 7 in.	36 oz.
	13 x 9 in.	48 oz.
	16 x 12 in.	72 oz.
Hearts • 4 in. high	6 in.	18 oz.
	8 in.	26 oz.
	9 in.	32 oz.
	10 in.	36 oz.
	12 in.	48 oz.
	14 in.	72 oz.
	16 in.	96 oz.
Petals • 4 in. high	6 in.	18 oz.
	9 in.	30 oz.
	12 in.	48 oz.
	15 in.	72 oz.
Squares • 4 in. high	6 in.	24 oz.
	8 in.	36 oz.
	10 in.	48 oz.
	12 in.	72 oz.
	14 in.	96 oz.
	16 in.	120 oz.
Hexagons • 4 in. high	6 in.	18 oz.
	9 in.	36 oz.
	12 in.	48 oz.
	15 in.	84 oz.
Contours • 3 in. high	9 in.	24 oz.

Recipes

Buttercream Icing

1/2 cup solid vegetable shortening
1/2 cup butter or margarine*
1 teaspoon clear vanilla extract
4 cups sifted confectioner's sugar (approx. 1 lb.)
2 tablespoons milk**

Cream butter and shortening with electric mixer. Add vanilla. Gradually add sugar, one cup at a time, beating well on medium speed. Scrape sides and bottom of bowl often. When all sugar has been mixed in, icing will appear dry. Add milk and beat at medium speed until light and fluffy. Keep bowl covered with a damp cloth until ready to use. For best results, keep icing bowl in refrigerator when not in use. Refrigerated in an airtight container, this icing can be stored 2 weeks. Rewhip before using. Makes 3 cups.

*Substitute all-vegetable shortening and 1/2 teaspoon Wilton No-Color Butter Flavor to create pure white icing with a stiffer consistency.

**Add 3-4 tablespoons light corn syrup per recipe to thin for icing cake smooth.

Royal Icing

3 tablespoons Meringue Powder
4 cups sifted confectioner's sugar (approx. 1 lb.)
6 tablespoons water***

Beat all ingredients at low speed for 7-10 minutes (10-12 minutes at high speed for portable mixer) until icing forms peaks. Makes 3 cups.

***When using large countertop mixer or for stiffer icing, use 1 tablespoon less water.

Rolled Fondant

Be sure to prepare and tint enough fondant to cover and decorate your cake. As with any icing, tint colors at one time; matching colors later may be difficult. Wilton also has convenient, Ready-To-Use Rolled Fondant, available in white, pastel, primary, neon and natural colors, for easy-to-handle fondant with no mixing.

2 envelopes or 1 tablespoon & 2 teaspoons unflavored gelatin
1/4 cup cold water
1/2 cup Wilton Glucose
2 tablespoons solid vegetable shortening
1 tablespoon Wilton Glycerin
Icing color and flavoring, as desired
8 cups sifted confectioner's sugar (about 2 lbs.)

Combine gelatin and cold water; let stand until gelatin is softened. Place gelatin mixture in top of double boiler and heat until dissolved. Add glucose; mix well. Stir in shortening and just before completely melted, remove from heat. Add glycerin, flavoring and color. Cool until lukewarm. Next, place 4 cups (1 pound) confectioner's sugar in a bowl and make a well. Pour the lukewarm gelatin mixture into the well and stir with a wooden spoon, mixing in sugar and adding more, a little at a time, until stickiness disappears. Knead in remaining sugar. Knead until the fondant is smooth, pliable and does not stick to your hands. If fondant is too soft, add more sugar; if too stiff, add water (a drop at a time). Use fondant immediately or store in airtight container in a cool, dry place. Do not refrigerate or freeze. When ready to use, knead again until soft. This recipe yields approximately 36 oz., enough to cover a 10 x 4 in. high round cake.

Chocolate Fondant

1 package (14 oz.) Dark Cocoa Candy Melts® brand confectionery coating
1/2 cup light corn syrup
24 oz. White Ready-to-Use Rolled Fondant
Brown Icing Color (optional)

Melt Candy Melts® according to package directions. Add corn syrup; stir to blend. Turn mixture out onto waxed paper; let stand at room temperature to dry and harden several hours. Wrap well and store at room temperature until ready to continue with recipe.

Knead small portions of candy mixture until soft and pliable. Knead softened mixture into fondant until smooth and evenly colored. If darker chocolate color is desired, knead in brown icing color.

Extra-Firm Rolled Fondant

For fondant with extra body and pliability—perfect for making drapes, swags and woven decorations.

1 to 2 teaspoons Gum-Tex™
24 oz. Wilton Ready-To-Use Rolled Fondant

Knead Gum-Tex into fondant until smooth. Store in an airtight container or tightly wrapped in plastic.

Thinned Fondant Adhesive

Use this mixture when attaching dried fondant to other fondant decorations or for attaching freshly-cut fondant pieces to lollipop sticks or florist wire.

1 oz. Wilton Ready-To-Use Rolled Fondant (1 1/2 in. ball)
1/4 teaspoon water

Knead water into fondant until it becomes softened and sticky. To attach a fondant decoration, place mixture in decorating bag fitted with a small round tip, or brush on back of decoration. Recipe may be doubled.

Working with Color

Combining several colors on your cake is part of the fun of fondant decorating. It's easy to tint white fondant just about *any color you can imagine using Wilton Icing Colors. Follow the chart on the next page to create your own custom colors.*

Tinting Fondant

Tint a small ball or enough to cover a whole cake—the important thing is to add just a little of the concentrated icing color at a time, until you arrive at the exact shade you want. If you'd rather not mix color yourself, Wilton also has pre-tinted fondant in a variety of pastel, primary, neon and natural shades.

1. Roll fondant into a ball, kneading until it's soft and pliable. Using a toothpick, add dots of icing color in several spots.

2. Knead color into your fondant ball; be sure to wear Wilton All-Purpose Decorating Gloves to keep your hands stain-free.

3. Continue kneading until color is evenly blended; add a little more color if needed.

Marbleizing

This subtle color treatment is an easy way to add richness to your cake. You can marbleize using white fondant with icing color or blend together white with our pre-tinted fondant.

Using Icing Color

1. Roll fondant into a ball, kneading until it's soft and pliable. Using a toothpick, add dots of icing color in several spots.

2. Knead fondant slightly until color begins to blend in, creating marbleized streaks. Roll out fondant to desired shape.

Using Pre-Tinted and White Fondant

1. Roll a log each of tinted and white fondant. Twist one log around the other several times.

2. Knead fondant slightly until color begins to blend in, creating marbleized streaks. Roll out fondant to desired shape.

Striping

Small strips of colored fondant can be rolled together to create a dazzling multi-colored fondant piece. It's a great way to make clothing, wrapped packages and other decorations stand out!

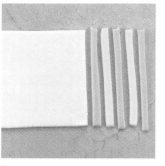

1. Roll out white fondant 1/8 in. thick and cut a base piece in desired size. Roll out various fondant colors 1/8 in. thick and cut strips in desired width.

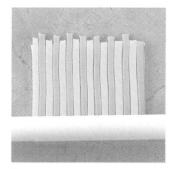

2. Position strips on white base, so that edges meet. Using rolling pin, evenly roll out piece to 1/8 in. thick, so that edges and layers blend together.

3. Cut striped piece to desired size.

Color Blending Chart

You've seen many exciting colors used in this book. But don't stop your imagination there! It's easy to blend your own custom colors using our Ready-To-Use Rolled Fondant (p. 114) in the combinations shown below. Combine our white and pre-tinted pastel, primary, neon and natural fondant shades

to get just the look you want. You can create school and sports team colors, match wedding or shower colors, produce business logos and much more. Just roll balls of fondant in the size recommended, knead together, then adjust as you wish, add more color to darken, more white to lighten.

Fondant Custom Color Palette

Use the combinations below to get the colors you want. 4 oz. of fondant equals a 2¹/₂ in. ball. Each mixture will produce between 4 and 5 oz. of fondant. Multiply as needed to cover a cake, using the chart on page 100.

Warm Gold

2¹/₂ in. primary yellow +
¹/₄ in. primary red

Buttercup Yellow

2¹/₂ in. white +
1 in. primary yellow +
¹/₄ in. natural dark brown

Ivory

2¹/₂ in. white +
¹/₂ in. natural dark brown +
¹/₂ in. primary yellow

Burnt Orange

2¹/₂ in. primary yellow +
¹/₂ in. primary red +
¹/₂ in. natural dark brown

Mauve

2¹/₂ in. white +
⁵/₈ in. neon pink +
¹/₄ in. natural black

Burgundy

2¹/₂ in. neon pink +
³/₄ in. natural black

Lilac

2¹/₂ in. white +
¹/₂ in. neon purple +
¹/₈ in. primary blue

Aqua

2¹/₂ in. white +
³/₄ in. primary blue +
⁵/₈ in. primary yellow

Sage Green

2¹/₂ in. white +
¹/₂ in. primary green +
¹/₈ in. natural black

Gray

2¹/₂ in. white +
¹/₂ in. natural black

Navy Blue

2¹/₂ in. primary blue +
⁵/₈ in. natural black

Bright Gold

2¹/₂ in. neon yellow +
¹/₂ in. neon orange

Templates for Rolling Fondant Balls

Use the circles here to roll balls to the size suggested in color mixing instructions. Just place your fondant ball on the template; add or remove fondant to arrive at the correct size.

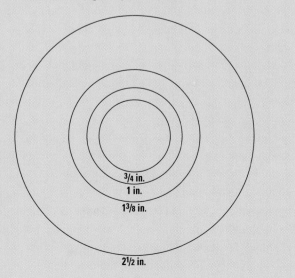
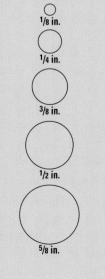

1/8 in.
1/4 in.
3/8 in.
1/2 in.
5/8 in.

3/4 in.
1 in.
1³/₈ in.
2¹/₂ in.

If Pastel Multi Packs are not available, use the following combinations.

Pastel Yellow

2¹/₂ in. white +
1³/₈ in. primary yellow

Pastel Blue

2¹/₂ in. white +
¹/₂ in. primary blue

Pastel Green

2¹/₂ in. white +
¹/₂ in. primary green

Pastel Pink

2¹/₂ in. white +
³/₈ in. primary red

Painting

Anyone can be an artist with rolled fondant! It's the ideal canvas for painting with thinned icing, Brush-On Color™ or Icing Writer. Use the Brush Set (p. 118) with its 3 different brush tip shapes to create a variety of exciting effects.

1. Large detail. Use the bevel tip brush to add bold details like leaves and petals and to create exciting shading effects.

2. Brush embroidery. This lace-look treatment for filling in flowers is easy to do with the square tip brush. Outline the flower with Icing Writer™ or thinned royal or buttercream icing, then immediately pull outlines toward the center with a damp brush.

3. Free-form designs. Dab on the color, for lively streamers, vines, confetti, scrolls, stars and other shapes. Use the round tip brush, along with a rainbow of Brush-On Colors, to make dots, messages, squiggles and more.

Marking with FoodWriters™

Use these edible color markers as you would an ink marker. Write messages, draw designs and add colorful details to fondant cut-outs. See page 116 for the selection of fine tip and bold tip FoodWriters in primary and neon colors.

1. Facial features. This is a great alternative to cutting features from fondant. Just use the bold tip FoodWriters to draw eyes, mouth and hair.

2. Messages. With fine tip FoodWriters, you can write or print letters in a rainbow of colors.

3. Finishing touches. Use bold and fine tip FoodWriters to draw stripes, dots and zigzags—great for detail on clothes, gifts, etc.

Stamping

There's no faster way to add colorful designs to your fondant cake! With our Cake Stamps™ and Brush-On Color™, you can cover a cake with fun shapes in minutes. To lighten Brush-On-Color, add a little White-White Icing Color, then stir to blend colors.

1. Pour Brush-On Color into Color Tray. Dip a stamp into the color. Stamp the design on parchment paper or a paper towel to test— you want to be sure the stamp is evenly covered with color before stamping on your cake.

2. Press stamp onto your cake, imprinting the design flat against the surface. If you want a design to run over the edge of your cake, stamp the top portion horizontally on your cake top, then while still touching the surface, pivot the

stamp to continue imprinting the design vertically. Rinse stamp in water whenever you change colors, then dry with paper towel.

3. Continue dipping and stamping until desired design is complete.

Sponging

This dappled color effect will work with Icing Writer™ or thinned royal or buttercream icing and crumpled paper towel. You can achieve different looks when you apply the color with crumpled waxed paper or plastic wrap.

1. Pour Icing Writer into Color Tray. Dip crumpled paper towel in the color. Test on parchment paper or a paper towel.

2. Lightly press against cake surface.

3. Continue sponging color until surface is covered. If some areas look too light, fill in with a little more color.

Brush Embroidery

Add textured flowers with the soft look of lace using this easy icing technique. Works best using the square tip brush from our Brush Set.

1. Imprint shape on freshly-rolled fondant (or on your covered cake), using a Cut-Out or cookie cutter.

2. Thin royal or buttercream icing with Piping Gel. Using tip 2, outline shape. For large designs, outline one section of the design, brush out lines following step 3, then continue with the next design section.

3. Before each outline can dry, immediately brush out lines of icing toward center of pattern area with damp brush. Work in quick, short strokes. Clean brush with water after brushing each flower to create distinct lines of icing.

4. Pipe tip 2 dot centers for flowers.

Color Accents

Make your fondant decorations shine by topping them with a sprinkle of Shimmer Dust™. This finely grained edible glitter gives flowers and greenery an elegant lustre.

1. Brush top of decoration with water.

2. Sprinkle top with Shimmer Dust right from the jar.

3. Shake off excess Shimmer Dust onto a piece of paper. Reserve for use on other designs.

Cutting and Shaping Techniques

You're ready to give cakes a whole new dimension with fondant decorations you cut out or form by hand. To attach your fondant piece to your fondant cake, you either brush *the back of the decoration lightly with water or with thinned fondant adhesive (p. 101).*

Cut-Outs

Fondant has a texture like roll-out cookie dough so it's perfect for cutting as you would a cookie. Use our Cut-Outs (p. 115), available in a wide range of designs, or your favorite cookie cutters.

1. Roll out fondant ⅛ in. thick on Roll & Cut Mat lightly dusted with cornstarch.

2. Cut out desired shapes, pressing your cutter evenly through the fondant.

3. Remove any excess fondant around the edges. Lift shape with a spatula. Position shape as needed.

Overlays

Many Cut-Outs or cookie cutter sets come in graduated shapes, making it easy to top one fondant shape with a smaller one. It's a great way to create fantasy flowers with different color centers.

1. Separately roll out 2 different colors of fondant, ⅛ in. thick, on Roll & Cut Mat lightly dusted with cornstarch.

2. Cut out desired shapes, using different size cutters. Remove any excess fondant around the edges. Lift shapes with a spatula.

3. Attach smaller shape to larger one with a damp brush.

Inlays

Using smaller Cut-Outs or cookie cutters, it's easy to inlay a contrasting color shape within a larger cut shape. Inlays can also be done directly on your fondant-covered cake—just cut out a shape, then replace it with the same size shape in a different color.

1. Separately roll out 2 different colors of fondant, ⅛ in. thick, on Roll & Cut Mat lightly dusted with cornstarch. Cut out shapes using different size cutters.

2. Using the smaller cutter, cut a shape from the center of your larger cut shape. Lift out the piece with a toothpick.

3. Position the contrasting color piece inside the opening in your larger shape. For large inlays, lightly smooth area with Easy-Glide Smoother; for small inlays, smooth seams with your fingertip.

Ribbons, Strips and Embossing

A smooth fondant surface always looks great on a cake, but you can also add subtle textures to fondant using our Fondant Ribbon Cutter/ Embosser (p. 117). This easy-to-use tool imprints elegant designs as it cuts fondant strips in a variety of widths and also imprints a beaded edge or textured striping. Our single-wheel Cutter/Embosser, used in the Quilting section below, is another great way to add a beautiful dimensional look to fondant cakes.

1. The Fondant Ribbon Cutter/ Embosser includes cutting wheels in straight, wavy and zigzag shapes, embossing wheels in striped and beaded styles, and spacers in multiple widths to help you adjust the width of the fondant strips. Arrange wheels on work surface to create the look you want. Place the cutting wheels to the outside of the embossing wheels. Add spacers between wheels to fill the width of the 4 in. roller*. Slide wheels and spacers on the roller.

2. Position washer and wing nut on end of roller to secure the wheels.

3. Use a rolling pin to roll out fondant on Roll & Cut Mat sprinkled with cornstarch. We suggest brushing the assembled roller with shortening for easy release. Roll the roller over fondant to cut and imprint strips. Attach strips to cake or make bows following instructions.

* Note: When using the beaded embossing wheel, load onto roller so that it fits over the center rim of the cutting wheel.

Fondant Punch Shapes

Adding exciting 3-dimensional decorations in fondant is easy with the Fondant Decorative Punch Set (p. 117). The comfortable angled handle holds your choice of 8 design punches from whimsical paisley to elegant teardrop flowers. This detailing will add variety and elegance to your cut out stripes or ribbons. Each disk cutout can be used as a separate fondant decoration or element. You can also create inlays of different fondant colors.

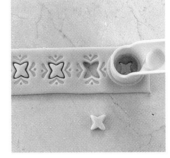

1. Insert desired disk on handle, twisting to lock into place. Roll out a strip of fondant on the Roll & Cut Mat sprinkled with cornstarch.

2. Dip disk in cornstarch, then press into fondant strip.

3. If the cut shape remains on the fondant strip, use a tapered spatula or toothpick to lift it out. If the shape lifts away with the disk, use the spatula to gently raise it from the disk. Position the fondant strip on your cake. Dip the disk in cornstarch before each pressing.

Quilting

By embossing lines in a lattice pattern, you will give your cake a great quilted look. Use the single-wheel Cutter/Embosser (p. 117) to create the imprinted lines. Quilting can be done on a cut fondant piece or directly on your fondant-covered cake. It's a textured look that's perfect for baby or garden-themed cakes.

1. Roll out fondant 1/8 in. thick on your Roll & Cut Mat sprinkled with cornstarch. Cut the desired size piece using the straight-edge wheel of the Cutter/ Embosser. (You may also create the quilted effect directly on your fondant-covered cake.) Lightly roll the Cutter/Embosser wheel over your cut piece to create diagonal lines. Use a small ruler and a straight edge to guide your wheel to space the lines evenly.

2. Roll the wheel in the opposite direction to create a diamond quilted pattern.

3. If needed, attach piece to cake using a damp brush.

Bows

Nothing says "celebrate" like a cake topped with a lush fondant bow. While the bow looks intricate, it's really just a grouping of fondant strips, folded, wrapped and arranged to create a full effect. When you cut strips with the Fondant Ribbon Cutter/Embosser (p. 117), you can create bows that have richly-textured, embossed designs.

1. Cut strips for bow loops and streamers, using dimensions listed in project instructions. Your bow may use more loops than shown here or it may omit the bow center. Cut ends of streamers in a v-shape; set streamers aside on waxed paper dusted with cornstarch. Fold strips over to form loops. Brush ends lightly with damp brush. Align ends and pinch slightly to secure. Stuff loops with crushed facial tissue. Let dry.

2. Cut strip for bow center, if needed, following dimensions in project instructions. Wrap strip around the ends of 2 loops to create a knot look, attaching with damp brush.

3. Attach streamers under loops with damp brush.

Curliques

You know how much flair curling ribbon adds to a package. Here's the easy way to make fondant curls. Curliques also are great used for hair, tails and confetti streamers.

1. Roll out fondant 1/16 in. thick on Roll & Cut Mat lightly dusted with cornstarch. Cut into thin strips.

2. Loosely wrap strips several times around a dowel rod to form curls. Let set 5 to 10 minutes.

3. Slide curl off dowel rod and let dry. Attach to cake with damp brush.

Ropes

The twisted texture is outstanding for cake borders. If you've ever piped a rope in buttercream icing, you'll really appreciate the flexibility and control you have with fondant.

1. Roll fondant into logs using palms of hands (see cake instructions for specific dimensions). You will need 2 pieces of the same length. Lay the pieces side by side, and gently press together at one end to join.

2. Holding the joined end in a stationary position, twist the other end 2 to 3 complete turns. Continue twisting as needed.

3. Attach rope to cake using a damp brush. Moisten cake slightly and position the rope, pressing ends lightly to secure.

4. For Multicolored Ropes: Follow Rope instructions for rolling individual logs, using 2 or 3 logs in different colors. Follow the same twisting procedure, but twist more loosely to create wider space between colors. After twisting, roll back and forth using palms of hands to create a smooth rope.

Draping

You can't do this with any other icing! The luxurious folds of a fondant drape add richness as a side garland or as skirt accents. Be sure not to roll fondant too thin—the weight of the drape may tear the ends.

1. Roll out fondant 1/8 in. thick on your Roll & Cut Mat lightly dusted with cornstarch. Cut rectangles in sizes and number stated in cake instructions.

2. Immediately gather the short ends and pinch together to form drapes. Trim ends with scissors to taper if needed.

3. Attach drapes to cake by brushing back with water.

Ruffles

A ruffle can be gently flowing or tightly gathered as shown here. To create a softer looking ruffle, after cutting your fondant section, roll the ball tool, dipped in cornstarch, along one edge.

1. Roll out fondant 1/8 in. thick on your Roll & Cut Mat lightly dusted with cornstarch. Cut a strip following size stated in cake instructions. As a general rule, you will need a strip 2 to 3 times the length of the size of the finished ruffle.

2. Starting on left side, fold small sections of the strip together vertically to form individual ruffles. As a section is done, continue adding strips by tucking cut end under the previous ruffle. Continue forming ruffles as needed.

3. Attach ruffle to cake by brushing top with water.

Figure Molding

Imagine creating replicas of your party guests in fondant! Or topping the kids' party cake with their favorite toys or animal shapes. It's easy when you use your hands to make some basic shapes. Follow the example of our fondant friend at right, modifying the head and body shapes and colors used to make the figures you want.

1. Shape the body parts. Roll a ball for head, a slightly flattened egg for chest and a rectangle for legs. Roll 2 small balls for shirt sleeves, indent using the ball tool from the Confectionery Tool Set. Roll 2 log arms, then flatten at end

and cut notch for thumb. Make ovals for shoes.

2. Attach pieces with a damp brush. Using a craft knife, cut a slit in the center of rectangle to make legs.

3. Draw facial features with fine tip FoodWriter™. Roll tiny balls for nose and ears, attach with damp brush. Make curliques for hair and attach with damp brush. Cut and attach a thin strip for belt and a small ball for buckle.

Leaves

Natural looking leaves can make your fondant bouquet come alive. Use the veining tool from the Confectionery Tool Set (p. 118) to mark vein lines and let leaves dry on flower formers to form a lifelike curved shape.

1. Roll out fondant ⅛ in. thick on your Roll & Cut Mat lightly dusted with cornstarch. Cut leaves using Cut-Outs™, cookie cutters or cutters from our gum paste decorating sets such as the Stepsaving Rose Bouquets Flower Cutter Set (p. 119).

2. Place leaf on thin foam. Using veining tool, mark vein lines, starting with center line. Add branch veins on both sides of center vein.

3. Remove leaf from foam and let dry. For curved leaves, dry on flower formers dusted with cornstarch.

Cupped Flowers

These little blossoms can go anywhere—on vines, as a side garland or on wires as part of a cake top bouquet. Make them ahead of time and let them dry in a pretty cupped shape.

  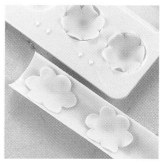

1. Roll out fondant ⅛ in. thick on Roll & Cut Mat lightly dusted with cornstarch. Cut flowers using Cut-Outs, cookie cutters or gum paste cutters. Transfer flowers one at a time to thin foam. Use ball tool from Confectionery Tool Set to soften edges by gently moving tool on edge of petal.

2. Transfer each flower to thick foam. Use ball tool or dog bone tool to form a cupped shape by depressing tool in center of flower.

3. Let flowers dry in flower formers dusted with cornstarch or in Candy Melting Plate sections. Add a tip 2 dot center using buttercream or royal icing or add a small ball of fondant for center.

Ribbon Roses

These quick and easy flowers can be placed on your cake right after you roll them. It's amazing how a few turns of your fondant strip can result in the realistic folds of a rose. Add fondant or buttercream leaves to create a full bouquet.

1. Roll out fondant ⅛ in. thick on Roll & Cut Mat lightly dusted with cornstarch. Cut a 1 x 5 in. strip.

2. Begin rolling lightly from one end, gradually loosening roll as flower gets larger. Fold cut edge under.

3. Trim flower to desired height with scissors.

Full Bloom Roses

This may be your proudest moment with fondant! When you can handshape a rose this realistic using simple cut-out shapes, you'll know fondant is the easiest icing for decorating a cake. Make sure to add 1 teaspoon Gum-Tex™ for each 12 oz. fondant so the petals stand up and curl properly.

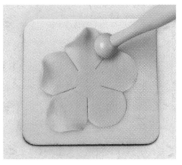

1. In advance: Make the rose center. Roll a ¹/2 in. ball of fondant and form into a teardrop shape. Coat the end of a toothpick with vegetable shortening, insert into bottom of rose center; let dry at least 24 hours.

2. Roll fondant ¹/16 in. thick on Roll & Cut Mat lightly dusted with cornstarch. Using the large rose cutter from the Stepsaving Set (p. 119), cut 3 blossom

shapes. Cover 2 of the blossoms with plastic wrap and set aside. On remaining blossom, use a spatula to make a ¹/2 in. cut between each petal toward middle of blossom. Place on thin foam and use ball tool from Confectionery Tool Set to soften edges of petals. Move blossom to thick foam and form a cup shape by pressing lightly in middle with ball tool.

3. Brush the middle of blossom with water. Insert the toothpick holding the rose center into the middle of the blossom and thread blossom up to the bottom of the rose center. Visualize the 5-petal blossom as a stick figure, with petals corresponding to "head," "arms" and "legs." Brush the "head" petal with water and wrap around rose center.

4. Brush one "arm" and opposite "leg" with water and fold up to cover the center bud. Repeat for remaining petals. Gently press bottom to shape. Pinch off any excess fondant from bottom. Furl back petal edges of the outer layer of petals.

5. Prepare the next blossom by making ¹/2 in. cuts between each petal.

Transfer to thin foam and use ball tool to soften petal edges. Transfer to thick foam and use ball tool to cup the 2 "arm" petals. Turn over blossom and cup 2 "leg" petals and "head" petal. Turn over blossom again and cup the center. Brush with water and thread onto toothpick. Brush the 2 "arm" petals

with water and attach, centering over the seams of the previous 2 petals.

6. Brush remaining petals with water and attach, spacing evenly. Press bottom to shape; pinch off excess if needed.

7. Prepare the last blossom by making ¹/2 in. cuts between each petal. Transfer to thin foam. Use ball tool to soften petal edges. Transfer to thick foam. Using the ball tool, cup all petals. Turn blossom shape over and cup center. Brush center with water. Thread

toothpick through the center of the blossom shape. Brush water inside petals as needed.

8. Turn rose over and let petals fall naturally into place. Gently press petals against the base to attach.

9. Roll out fondant ¹/16 in. thick and cut calyx using calyx cutter from the Stepsaving Set. Brush base of calyx with water and thread toothpick through center of calyx. Press to attach and let dry. Remove from toothpick.

Boombox Display Panel *(see "Booming Out The Tunes", p. 46)*

How to Use Patterns

The patterns shown here are used as guides for cutting or decorating specific fondant accents in this book. For all patterns, except the Soccer Ball, follow these steps:

1. Roll out fondant to thickness stated in project directions.

2. Cut out pattern and position on fondant. Trace pattern with toothpick.

3. Cut out piece using a craft knife.

For Soccer Ball, cut fondant ball following project directions. Trace pattern onto waxed paper. Position waxed paper pattern on cut ball; using toothpick, carefully imprint along pattern lines to transfer a dotted line of pattern onto ball. Draw in seams with FoodWriter.

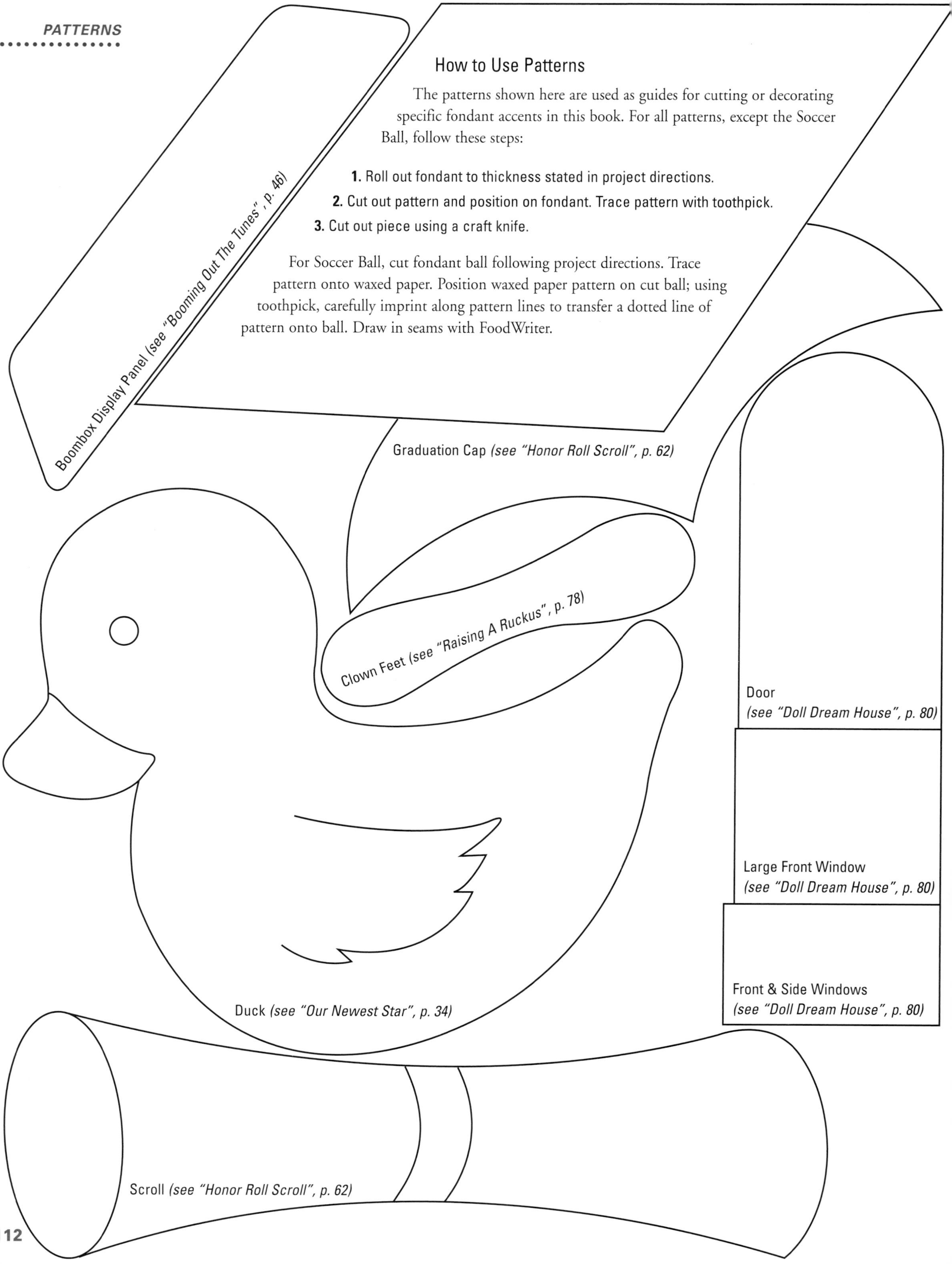

Graduation Cap *(see "Honor Roll Scroll", p. 62)*

Clown Feet *(see "Raising A Ruckus", p. 78)*

Door
(see "Doll Dream House", p. 80)

Large Front Window
(see "Doll Dream House", p. 80)

Front & Side Windows
(see "Doll Dream House", p. 80)

Duck *(see "Our Newest Star", p. 34)*

Scroll *(see "Honor Roll Scroll", p. 62)*

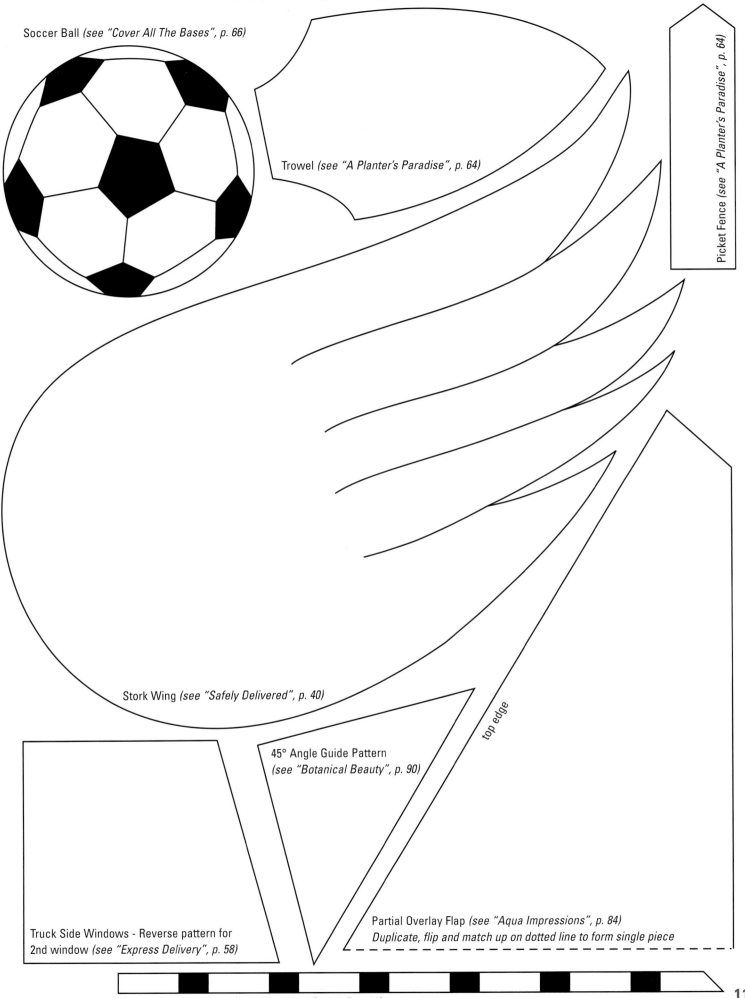

Soccer Ball *(see "Cover All The Bases", p. 66)*

Trowel *(see "A Planter's Paradise", p. 64)*

Picket Fence *(see "A Planter's Paradise", p. 64)*

Stork Wing *(see "Safely Delivered", p. 40)*

45° Angle Guide Pattern
(see "Botanical Beauty", p. 90)

top edge

Truck Side Windows - Reverse pattern for
2nd window *(see "Express Delivery", p. 58)*

Partial Overlay Flap *(see "Aqua Impressions", p. 84)*
Duplicate, flip and match up on dotted line to form single piece

Lattice Spacing Pattern *(see "Botanical Beauty", p. 90)*

Fondant Decorating Products

Here's just a sample of the great Wilton products that make your fondant decorating easy! Wilton is the world's #1 cake decorating resource, with the finest bakeware, baking tools, decorating tips, ingredients, cake toppers and more. To find our complete selection, including all the Wilton products included in the Checklist for each project, see your Wilton dealer, our annual Wilton Yearbook of Cake Decorating, or our website: www.wilton.com.

Ready-To-Use-Rolled Fondant

Fondant has never been more convenient and fun for decorating! With Wilton Ready-To-Use Rolled Fondant, the color is already mixed in for kneading, no mess, no guesswork. The 24 oz. (1$^{1}/_{2}$ lb.) package, available in white and pastel colors, covers an 8 in. 2-layer cake plus decorations; the 80 oz. package (5 lbs.), available in white only, covers a 2-layer 6 in., 8 in. and 10 in. round tiered cake plus decorations. Certified Kosher.

White
24 oz. (1$^{1}/_{2}$ lb.) Pk.
710-2076

White
80 oz. (5 lb.) Pk.
710-2180

Pastel Pink
24 oz. (1$^{1}/_{2}$ lb.) Pk.
710-2181

Pastel Blue
24 oz. (1$^{1}/_{2}$ lb.) Pk.
710-2182

Pastel Yellow
24 oz. (1$^{1}/_{2}$ lb.) Pk.
710-2183

Pastel Green
24 oz. (1$^{1}/_{2}$ lb.) Pk.
710-2184

Fondant Multi Packs

Primary Colors
Green, Red, Yellow, Blue
17.6 oz. (Four 4.4 oz. pouches) Pk.
710-445

Neon Colors
Purple, Orange, Yellow, Pink
17.6 oz. (Four 4.4 oz. pouches) Pk.
710-446

Pastel Colors
Blue, Yellow, Pink, Green
17.6 oz. (Four 4.4 oz. pouches) Pk.
710-447

Natural Colors
Light Brown, Dark Brown, Pink, Black
17.6 oz. (Four 4.4 oz. pouches) Pk.
710-448

Cut Outs

With Cut-Outs, it's easy to make fun 3-D shapes for your fondant cakes and cupcakes. Just roll out fondant, press down with cut-out and lift away. Remove shapes with a small spatula.

Stainless steel shapes range from 5/8 in. to 2 1/2 in.

- Fast, fun way to brighten any fondant cake!
- Great assortments of shapes for any occasion.
- Perfect for highlighting with Brush-On Color™ or Icing Writer™.

Look what you can do!

1. Layered decorations!

2. Fondant fill-in!

3. Cake insets!
See p. 106.

Square
417-431 Set/3

Round
417-432 Set/3

Star
417-433 Set/3

Heart
417-434 Set/3

Flower
417-435 Set/3

Funny Flower
417-436 Set/3

Leaf
417-437 Set/3

Oval
417-438 Set/3

People
417-441 Set/6

Garden Shapes
Butterfly, Tulip, Bell, Flower
417-443 Set/4

Crinkle Shapes
Circle, Square, Triangle, Heart
417-444 Set/4

Fancy Shapes
Flower, Leaf. Oval, Heart
417-445 Set/4

Alphabet/Number
417-442 Set/37

Daisy
Durable plastic
417-439 Set/3

Brush-on Color™

Ready-to-use edible decorating paint adds a vivid finish to fondant shapes! Just pour into the Color Tray (p. 118), then brush on or stamp on your fondant-covered cake. In seconds, you can add brilliant designs in a rainbow of bright colors.

3 oz. bottles.
Certified Kosher.

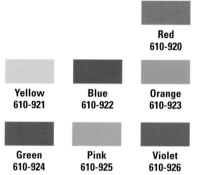

	Red 610-920
Yellow 610-921	Blue 610-922	Orange 610-923
Green 610-924	Pink 610-925	Violet 610-926

Icing Writer™

Squeeze on colorful accents—flowers, swirls, messages and more—with this ready-to-use icing! It's easy to control for precise decorating: Just squeeze the bottle and icing flows easily from the built-in round tip. Trace imprinted shapes made with Cut-Outs or draw dazzling freehand designs. Dries to a smooth, satin finish. Product can be thinned by placing bottle in hot water for 5 minutes

3 oz. bottles.
Certified Kosher.

	Red 710-2225
Yellow 710-2226	Blue 710-2227	White 710-2228
Green 710-2229	Pink 710-2230	Violet 710-2231

FoodWriter™ Edible Color Markers

Use like ink markers to add fun and dazzling color to countless foods. Kids love 'em! Decorate on fondant, Color Flow, royal icing, even directly on cookies. Brighten everyday foods like toaster pastries, cheese, fruit slices, bread and more.

Each set includes five .35 oz. FoodWriter pens.
Certified Kosher.

Primary Colors

Yellow	Green	Red	Blue	Black

Fine Tip 609-100 Set/5   **Bold Tip** 609-115 Set/5

Neon Colors

Purple	Orange	Pink	Light Green	Black

Fine Tip 609-116 Set/5

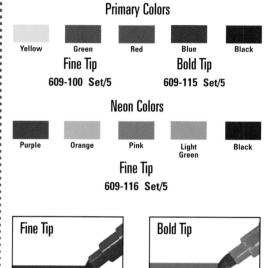

Fine Tip   Bold Tip

Shimmer Dust™

Give your fondant decorating that added dash of color! Sprinkle on Shimmer Dust—the sparkling color will give your decorations a jolt of excitement your guests will love. Just brush your fondant-covered cake top or fondant Cut-Outs with water and sprinkle lightly over the dampened area.

.47 oz. Certified Kosher.

Elegant
Silver, Gold, Pearl
703-212 Set/3

Bright
Pink, Yellow, Orange
703-211 Set/3

Primary
Red, Green, Blue
703-210 Set/3

Cake Stamps™

Stamp colorful designs onto your fondant-covered cakes, cupcakes or cookies—it's easy and fun!

Shapes range from 1 to 1½ in.

- Four exciting stamp sets, each with six lively designs!
- Food-safe, with convenient handles for even imprinting.
- Use with Brush-On Color and Color Tray to create brilliant shapes!

Geometric
Star, Square, Square Border, Triangle, Round, Heart
417-181 Set/6

Nature
Tulip, Bee, 5-Petal Flower, 6-Petal Flower, Butterfly, Leaf
417-182 Set/6

Romantic
Champagne Glass, Spiral, Dove Left, Dove Right, Bow, Bell
417-183 Set/6

Baby
Rattle, Bear, Duck, Carriage, Frame, Shoe
417-184 Set/6

Fondant Ribbon Cutter/Embosser Set

This easy-to-use tool is the perfect way to add beautiful textured fondant ribbons, stripes and bows to your cake. Just choose the cutting and embossing wheel designs you want, slide the washer, core, wheels and spacers on the roller handle, and roll on top of your fondant. We suggest brushing the assembled roller with shortening for easy release. The perfectly cut ribbon strips are ready to place right on your cake! Produces ribbon widths from $1/4$ in. to $3^3/4$ in. when combining spacers.

1907-1203 Set/26
Complete set includes:
- 9 cutting wheels—3 straight, 3 wavy, 3 zigzag
- 8 embossing wheels—4 striped, 4 beaded
- 9 spacers—one $1/3$ in., two each $1/4$, $1/2$, $3/4$ and 1 in. wide
- Roller handle detachable core
- Assembly hardware

Embossing Wheels · Cutting Wheels · Spacers

Use spacers to create the perfect ribbon width!

4 Beaded · 4 Striped · 3 Straight · 3 Wavy · 3 Zigzag

Emboss striped and beaded textures!
Cut zigzag, wavy and straight edges!

Just Load and Roll!

1. Arrange wheels on work surface to create the look you want.

2. Slide wheels and spacers on the roller.

3. Position washer and wing nut on end of roller to secure the wheels.

4. Use a Rolling pin to roll out fondant on your Roll & Cut Mat. Roll the roller over fondant in any direction.

Fondant Decorative Punch Set

Add exciting 3-dimensional decorations in fondant with this easy-to-use tool. In seconds, you can punch out fondant accents with elegant openwork shapes like diamonds and flowers. As you punch, the disk imprints a detailed design that adds a pretty touch of texture to any cake. The comfortable angled handle holds your choice of 8 design disks. Also great for adding fondant detail to cupcakes and cookies. Disks turn to lock into place.

1907-1204 Set/9

| Large Tulip with Leaves | Dutch Blossom | Paisley with Dots | Wide Diamond with Scrolls |
| Small Tulip with Leaves | Snapdragon with Leaves | 4-Leaf Clover with Dots | Narrow Diamond with Scrolls |

Fondant Tools and Accessories

Perfect Height™ Rolling Pin

Roll out fondant evenly, at the perfect thickness for easy cutting and shaping, with this non-stick roller. Roll to the perfect $1/8$ in. height used for cutting many fondant decorations, using the slide-on guide rings. This rolling pin is easy to handle—just the right size for preparing small amounts of fondant to place on your cake. Perfect for use with Fondant Multi Packs and Cut-Outs™! 9 x 1 in. diameter.

1907-1205

Wide Glide™ Rolling Pin

Its extra-wide, smooth design is perfect for covering cakes with rolled fondant. The non-stick surface makes handling large pieces of fondant easy—just dust the surface with confectioner's sugar and roll out fondant to the size you need, then use the Wide Glide Rolling Pin to lift the fondant from your work surface to the cake. Great for rolling out pastry dough and pie crusts, too. 20 x 1$1/2$ in. diameter.

1907-1210

Contour Pan

Create cakes with an elegant, rounded top edge. This is the perfect shape for positioning rolled fondant. One-mix pan is 9 x 3 in. deep. Aluminum.

2105-6121

Roll & Cut Mat

For precise measuring, rolling and cutting of fondant or dough. Pre-marked circles for exact sizing. Square grid helps you cut precise strips. Non-stick surface for easy release.

409-412

Easy-Glide Fondant Smoother

Essential tool for shaping and smoothing rolled fondant on your cake. Works great on top, edges and sides! Shapes fondant to sides of cake so that no puffed areas appear. Trim any excess with a sharp knife. 6 $1/4$ in. long x 3 $1/4$ in. wide.

1907-1200

Color Tray

Become a true fondant artist with this convenient tray! Pour in Brush-On Color and use Cake Stamps or the Brush Set to add vivid designs to fondant cakes.

1907-1208

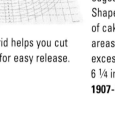

Brush Set

Add a special touch of color to your fondant-covered cake! It's easy and fun with these fine-bristle brushes and Brush-On Color or Icing Writer. Three tip designs—round, square and bevel—help you achieve different painted effects. Also great for attaching fondant decorations with water or thinned fondant.

1907-1207 Set/3

Candy Melting Plate

Great for drying fondant flowers. Microwave—melt up to 11 Candy Melts®* colors at one time for less mess. Plastic with non-slip grip edge. Includes decorating brush.

1904-8016

*Brand confectionery coating.

Quick Ease Roller

Makes it easy to prepare small pieces of fondant and gum paste for cutting flowers and designs. Wooden roller fits comfortably in palm of hand.

1907-1202

Cutter/Embosser

Three detachable wheels—straight, wavy and ridged—for cutting and for embossing of patterns on fondant. Light, easy-rolling design cuts at the perfect angle. Comfortable handle also stores wheels.

1907-1206

Flower Former Set

Dry fondant or icing leaves and flowers in a convex or concave shape. Three each of 1$1/2$, 2 and 2$1/2$ in. wide holders, all 11 in. long.

417-9500 Set/9

Confectionery Tool Set

Invaluable tools for shaping, imprinting and stenciling—helping you achieve lifelike fondant or gum paste flowers. Ideal for marking patterns in fondant cakes, shaping marzipan fruits. Includes plastic Dogbone, Umbrella, Shell, Ball and Veining tools.

1907-1000 Set/5

Fondant Shaping Foam

Thick and thin squares are the ideal soft surface for shaping flowers, leaves and other fondant or gum paste cutouts. Use the thin square for thinning petal edges with a ball tool, carving vein lines on leaves and making ruffled fondant strips. Use the thick square for cupping flower centers. Thin 4 x 4 x $1/8$ in. Thick 4 x 4 x 1 in.

1907-9704

Fondant and Gum Paste Decoration Sets

Floral Collection Flower Making Set

Make incredibly lifelike gum paste flowers. Full-color how-to book includes many arranging ideas and step-by-step instructions. Kit includes 24 plastic cutters, 1 leaf mold, 3 wood modeling tools, protector flap, 40-page instruction book and 2 foam squares for modeling.
1907-117 Set/32
Book only 907-117

Floral Garland Cutter/Ejector Set

Quickly and easily cuts and positions fondant or gum paste flowers on cakes. Includes ejector, 5 cutters and instructions.
1907-1001 Set/7

Stepsaving Rose Bouquets Flower Cutter Set

Create gorgeous fondant and gum paste roses and forget-me-nots using cutters and book in this set. Cutters include large and small rose, rose leaf, calyx and forget-me-not.
1907-1003 Set/6

Icings

All Wilton icings are formulated for decorating as well as taste. That's because Wilton insists on providing you with the perfect consistency icing for decorating. Our quality ingredients mean better results for you.

Ready-To-Use Decorator Icings

Wilton makes the only ready-to-use icing that is the perfect consistency for decorating. Delicious taste, too. One can covers two 8 or 9 in. layers or one 9 x 13 in. cake.
16 oz.
White 710-118
Chocolate 710-119

Creamy White Buttercream Icing Mix

Our convenient mix has the delicious taste and creamy texture of homemade buttercream icing— enough to ice a 1-layer 8 in. cake. Use just as you would your favorite buttercream recipe. Makes 1½ to 2 cups. Certified Kosher.
710-112

Fondant and Gum Paste Ingredients

Glycerin

Stir into dried out fondant, gum paste and icing color to restore consistency.
2 oz. Certified Kosher.
708-14

Glucose

Essential ingredient for making fondant and gum paste from scratch. Use with Wilton Gum-Tex™.
12 oz.
707-107

Gum-Tex™

Makes fondant and gum paste pliable, elastic, easy to shape. Flip-top can has a plastic resealable lid.
6 oz.
707-117

Gum Paste Mix

Just add water and knead. Workable, pliable dough-like mixture molds into beautiful flowers and figures.
1 lb.
707-124

No-Color Flavorings

Decorators trust Wilton flavorings for great taste that won't change icing consistency. Wilton flavors are concentrated–only a drop or two adds delicious taste to icings, cakes, beverages and other recipes. Recommended by and used in Wilton Method Classes, these delicious flavors won't change your icing color. Essential for making pure white icings for wedding cakes and maintaining vibrant colors in all your decorating. Certified Kosher.

Clear Vanilla Extract
2 oz.
604-2237
8 oz.
604-2269

No-Color Butter Flavor
2 oz.
604-2040
8 oz.
604-2067

No-Color Almond Extract
2 oz.
604-2126

Keeping In Touch With Wilton...

There's always something new at Wilton! Fun decorating courses that will help your decorating skills soar. Exciting cake designs to challenge you. Great new decorating products to try. Helpful hints to make your decorating more efficient and successful. Here's how you can keep up to date with what's happening at Wilton.

Decorating Classes

Do you want to learn more about cake decorating, with the personal guidance of a Wilton instructor? Wilton has two ways to help you.

The Wilton School of Cake Decorating and Confectionery Art is the home of the world's most popular cake decorating system—The Wilton Method. For more than 75 years, thousands of students from around the world have learned to decorate cakes using the techniques featured in The Wilton Method. In 1929, Dewey McKinley Wilton taught the first small classes in the kitchen of his Chicago home. Today, The Wilton School teaches more people to decorate than any school in the world. As the school has grown, some techniques have been refined and there are more classes to choose from—but the main philosophies of the Wilton Method have remained.

The Wilton School occupies a state-of-the-art facility in Darien, Illinois. More than 90 courses are offered each year, including The Master Course, a 2-week class that provides individualized instruction in everything from borders and flowers to constructing a tiered wedding cake. Other courses focus on specific decorating subjects, such as Lambeth and Cakes for Catering. Courses in Gum Paste and Chocolate Artistry feature personal instruction from well-known experts in the field.

For more information or to enroll, write to:
School Secretary
Wilton School of Cake Decorating and Confectionery Art
2240 West 75th Street, Woodridge, IL 60517.

Or call: 630-810-2211 for a free brochure and schedule.

Wilton Class Programs are the convenient way to learn to decorate, close to your home. Our Wilton Method Classes are easy and fun for everyone. You can learn the fundamentals of cake decorating with a Wilton-trained teacher in just four 2-hour classes. When the course is over, you'll know how to decorate star and shell birthday cakes or floral anniversary

cakes like a pro. Everyone has a good time — it's a great place for new decorators to discover their talent. Since 1974, hundreds of thousands have enjoyed these courses. Special Project Classes are also available in subjects like candy-making, gingerbread, fondant, cookie blossoms and more.

Call 800-942-8881 for class locations and schedules.

Wilton Products

Visit a Wilton Dealer near you. Your local Wilton Dealer is the best place to see the great variety of cake decorating products made by Wilton. If you are new to decorating, it's a good idea to see these products in person; if you are an experienced decorator, you'll want to visit your Wilton Dealer regularly to have the supplies you need on hand. From bakeware and icing supplies to candles and publications, most Wilton retailers carry a good stock of items needed for decorating. Remember, the selection of products changes with each season, so if you want to decorate cakes in time for upcoming holidays, visit often to stock up on current pans, colors and toppers.

Order on-line, by phone or by mail.
You can also place orders 24 hours a day at our website, www.wilton.com. Shopping on-line is fast, easy and secure. Or, you can place an order by phone at 800-794-5866 (7WILTON) or by mail, using the Order Form in the Wilton Yearbook of Cake Decorating.

Wilton On The Web

www.wilton.com is the place to find Wilton decorating information on-line. Looking for a fun new cake to make? Our website is filled with great decorating ideas, updated regularly to fit the season. Need a recipe? www.wilton.com has delicious desserts and icings to try. Want to save decorating time? There are always helpful hints and answers to common decorating questions. You can also discover new Wilton products and shop for your favorites at www.wilton.com.

Wilton Publications

We never run out of decorating ideas! Each year, Wilton publishes more new idea books based on Wilton Method techniques. When you're planning a specific occasion, Wilton books are a fantastic source of decorating inspiration.

The Wilton Yearbook of Cake Decorating
is our annual showcase of the latest ideas in decorating. Each edition is packed with all-new cake ideas, instructions and products — it's the best place to find out what's new at Wilton. Cakes for every occasion throughout the year are here: holidays, graduations, birthdays, weddings and more. If you are looking for a new cake to test your decorating skills, you can't beat the Yearbook.

Wilton also regularly publishes special interest decorating books, including books on wedding and holiday decorating, candy-making, home entertaining and food gifting. Look for them wherever Wilton products are sold.